THE INSPIRATION OF THE HOLY SPIRIT

THE INSPIRATION OF THE HOLY SPIRIT

Dr. Echol Lee Nix, Sr.
with Dr. Echol Lee Nix, Jr.
and Mrs. Annie Mae Nix

NewSouth Books
Montgomery

NewSouth Books
P.O. Box 1588
Montgomery, AL 36102

Library of Congress Cataloging-in-Publication Data

Nix, Echol Lee, Sr.
The inspiration of the Holy Spirit / Echol Lee Nix, Sr. with Echol Lee Nix, Jr. and Annie Mae Nix.

p. cm.

ISBN-13: 978-1-60306-121-6 (trade paper)
ISBN-10: 1-60306-121-5 (trade paper)
Also issued in limited release hardcover

1. Christian life—Biblical teaching. 2. Bible—Meditations. I. Nix, Echol Lee. II. Nix, Annie Mae. III. Title.
BS680.C47N59 2011
248.4—dc23

2011035291

Design by Brian Seidman
Printed in the United States of America

This book is dedicated to the memories of

MR. EARNEST NIX

MRS. REBETHAR LEE NIX

MRS. EARNESTINE JACKSON

the author's father, mother, and sister, respectively.

Contents

About the Author

The REVEREND DR. ECHOL LEE NIX, SR. is a distinguished educator, counselor, former pastor, and evangelist. At an early age, he learned the valuable lessons of hard work, commitment, dedication, and sacrifice. Although he came from rural and humble beginnings in Montevallo, Alabama, he never used his background as an excuse to fail but rather as an opportunity to succeed. Before leaving home, he held several paraprofessional jobs such as a yard boy, janitor, collector, and salesman. Always setting his sights higher than what others said or expected of him, he continued to explore options and took advantage of new and different opportunities along the way. After graduating from Montevallo High School in Montevallo, Alabama, he attended Mississippi Valley State University with a football scholarship. While in college, he was awarded an Air Force ROTC scholarship and the Howard Thurman Academic Scholarship.

Dr. Nix, Sr. received a Bachelor of Science degree in Health, Physical Education and Recreation, with military and academic honors. During the graduation ceremony, he received a commission in the United States Air Force, and moved to Montgomery, Alabama to become an education and training officer. Later, Dr. Nix received a Master of Education degree, "AA" professional teaching certificate, Education Specialist degree, and a Master of Education certification in Administration—all from Alabama State University. In 1984, he accepted a call to the ministry and was convinced that the call to ministry is a call to preparation. Therefore, he earned a Bachelor of Theology degree, was awarded a Doctor of Divinity degree for excellence in education and community service, and earned the Ph.D. in Pastoral Counseling Psychology from the Christian Bible College and Seminary in Independence, Missouri. Additional schools attended were: Air Force Institute of Technology, Samford University (Montgomery, Alabama Extension), Texas A & M University, and Florida State University.

Moreover, Dr. Nix, Sr. has held several positions in education at the secondary and collegiate levels. He served as an instructor and chairman of the Driver Education program at Carver High School and Robert E. Lee High School, respectively, before retiring from the Montgomery County Public School System in June 2001. He has also held teaching positions with the Montgomery Driving School, Texas A & M University, and Alabama State University. Dr. Nix, Sr. has served as a Master Teacher in Driver Education for the Alabama State Department of Education. During the Clinton Administration, he was asked to serve as an ambassador to Japan and South Africa as one of the thirty experts in Driver Education. He co-authored two books in Driver Education for the state of Alabama. In addition, Dr. Nix, Sr. has many published poems and editorials in several periodicals. He has been listed four times in *Who's Who Among the Best Students and Teachers*. Dr. Nix, Sr. served for five years as pastor of Pilgrim Missionary Baptist Church in Ramer, Alabama. He taught as a professor of theology at Selma University in Selma, Alabama for three years. Dr. Nix, Sr. was married to Mrs. Annie Mae Nix for thirty-nine years and together they raised Pamela, Echol Jr., Keturah and Earnest. One of his favorite scriptures is Philippians 4:13: "I can do all things through Christ who strengthens me."

About the Co-Authors

The REVEREND DR. ECHOL LEE NIX, JR. is the second child born to the Rev. Dr. Echol and Mrs. Annie Nix in Jefferson County, Alabama. He graduated from George Washington Carver High School and later Morehouse College in Atlanta, Georgia. While at Morehouse, he accepted a call to the ministry and was licensed at nineteen years old and ordained at twenty-one. During his college years, he was a Congressional Intern, working in the United States House of Representatives (Washington, D.C.) and traveled to Hong Kong and Singapore as a student ambassador.

He received the Master of Divinity degree from Vanderbilt University (Nashville, TN) and served as an associate minister at Baptist and Cumberland Presbyterian Churches in the Nashville area. He also participated in a study course in the Holy Land to better understand the history and geography of the Bible and visited biblical cities, including Bethlehem, Jerusalem, Jericho, Joppa, and Galilee.

After Vanderbilt, Dr. Nix, Jr. pursued a year of further study at Princeton Theological Seminary (Princeton, NJ) and then enrolled at Boston University. In 2000, he was awarded a second master's degree in Theology and the Ph.D. degree (2007), both from Boston University. Because of Dr. Nix, Jr.'s academic work and community service, he was awarded an international fellowship anywhere in the world. He chose Frankfurt am Main, Germany and lived and studied in Europe for three years, traveling throughout Germany and France. While in Germany, he participated in many social and religious activities. He taught bible study and preached at German Protestant churches and delivered a public lecture at Frankfurt University. He writes in the areas of theology and religion and has published several articles in periodicals and professional literature. His book, *Ernst Troeltsch and Comparative Theology*, contributes to an emerging field of religious study, namely comparative theology and theologies of religious pluralism.

Dr. Nix, Jr. is an Assistant Professor in the Department of Religion at Furman University, Greenville, South Carolina. He serves on the Board of the Baptist World

Alliance (Commission on Ethics) and is an officer of the North American Paul Tillich Society. He is ordained in the National Baptist Church and is married to the former Rosetia Johnson of Montgomery, Alabama. They are the proud parents of McKenzie Grace.

MRS. ANNIE MAE NIX was an amazing and wonderful woman. She inspired countless people with her powerful testimony and her personal example of courage, faith, and hope. She had the ability to "walk with kings and queens but did not lose the common touch." She was a pillar of strength for her family, for her church, and for her community. In fact, Mrs. Nix was an inspiration to all. She not only "talked the talk" of being a faithful believer, she "walked the walk" by loving God with all her heart, mind, and soul and by living a good life through dedicated service to others. She was the kind of person King Solomon had in mind when he described a virtuous woman as "more precious than rubies and who reaches her hand out to the needy. Her children rise up and call her blessed; her husband also, and he praises her."

Mrs. Nix's early childhood was spent in Montevallo, Alabama where she was raised by her parents, Mr. Willie James and Mrs. Willie Mae Moore. She attended Almont Elementary, Prentice and Montevallo High School. While living in Montevallo, she was a member of the Everdale (now New Everdale) Baptist Church and was baptized into the Christian faith by Reverend G. C. Massey. She continued her work in the church under Reverend W. H. Lee and participated in church auxiliaries and many youth and young adult programs. After marrying Rev. Dr. Nix, Sr. she moved to Montgomery, Alabama and they began a new life together with a growing family while he completed graduate school and post-graduate studies. They joined Beulah Baptist Church in Hope Hull, Alabama and later Dr. Nix, Sr. was called to pastor Pilgrim Baptist Church in Ramer, Alabama. As a first lady, she served with an unusual amount of dedication and grace. After leaving Pilgrim, she united with Hall Street Baptist Church in Montgomery, Alabama, and was active in several activities, such as the Matrons and the Ministers Wives Circle of Montgomery.

Mrs. Nix was publicly recognized for her courage and determination in spite of her health challenges. She was featured twice in the *Montgomery Advertiser* with front page articles as the cover story. She was also featured in the *Montgomery-Tuskegee Times* newspaper and was featured on television Channel 7 (KATV) News in Little Rock, Arkansas. The title of the television segment was "Look Good, Feel Better," and she was hand-picked by Mary Kay representatives for a public makeover because of her "inner personality, beauty and class."

Mrs. Nix saw hope when others saw despair and the shining light of God's grace was all over her. She was the kind of person Saint Matthew had in mind when he wrote: "Do not put your light under a bushel, but on a candlestick." Mrs. Annie Nix was like a candle in the dark. In her own words, she agreed with the songwriter and often said, "This little light of mine, I'm going to let it shine, let it shine, let it shine, let it shine."

Acknowledgments

The authors would like to express their sincere gratitude and appreciation to several people who offered valuable suggestions and relentless encouragement during the writing phase of this volume. Being cognizant of the fact that behind every author stand a number of people who have assisted indirectly through inference, influence, direct contact or by means of technological assistance. Books are never the achievement of one author.

We are indebted to the insights of immediate family members who were instrumental during the early stages of this book's development. First, Mrs. Annie Mae Nix deserves special mention. She was a loving wife and mother and was instrumental in this book's origin and development. Not only was she patient and understanding as the sermons were being revised for publication but she agreed to be a contributing writer. Her faithfulness and support were extended through the years as we traveled many places and preached the Gospel. Appreciation is also extended to Mrs. Rosetia Johnson Nix and McKenzie Grace Nix for their understanding during the long hours of writing and editing. Faculty and staff in the Religion

Department at Furman University in Greenville, South Carolina are acknowledged for their strong support, assistance, and understanding.

Furthermore, we acknowledge Mr. Glenn Jackson and his family for their dedication and generosity exemplified through the years. We also wish to thank Mrs. Pamela Anita Bradshaw and Miss Keturah Nix for the onerous task of deciphering our handwriting and transforming it in a type-written manuscript. Mr. Earnest Nix, Sr., Mrs. Rosie Nix, and Captain Ray Bradshaw are thanked as well for their love and kindness demonstrated while writing this book.

In addition, we are grateful for the insights of Reverend W. H. Lee, former pastor of the Everdale Baptist Church; Reverend William D. Walker, pastor of the New Everdale Baptist Church (Montevallo, Alabama); and church members for giving us the opportunity to follow such marvelous leadership. Coach and Mrs. Jimmy Jones, two of Montevallo's legendary greats must be mentioned. While the author was growing up, they stimulated and motivated him on and off the football field to be the best.

Further, we lovingly remember Reverend Dr. Fred D. Matthews, a faithful "father in the ministry," who was the Religious Coordinator at Mississippi Valley State University and pastor of New Bethel Baptist Church (Itta Bena, Mississippi).

Sincere appreciation is also extended to Rev. Dr. Frank R. Johnson who served as a great teacher and mentor. The love, kindness and friendship of Pastor Eric Galbreath and Mrs. Renita Galbreath, and members of the Hall Street Missionary Baptist Church will be forever remembered and cherished.

Special thanks is extended to Reverend Ricky Perdue and Minister Jackie Perdue, Reverend Artis Clayton and Mrs. Jacquelyn Clayton for encouraging us to complete this book, as well as Mr. John P. Brown, Jr., for his editorial assistance and suggestions. We are also grateful to all of our current and former students. Our students have been a blessing, in many ways, as well as a source of motivation.

We gratefully acknowledge Mr. Randall Williams and Mr. Brian Seidman of New South Books for their professionalism and interest in this publication. They have been encouraging and supportive throughout the whole process and gave excellent instructions with the book's specifications. Finally, we thank God for enabling us to complete one of our life-long goals.

Foreword

Dr. Echol L. Nix, Jr.

In times like these—where we often hear bad news and reports—humanity is in need of assurance, hope, and comfort. This book attempts to offer good news and inspiring messages to uplift the human spirit. One of the underlying theses throughout all these pages is that humanity is flawed and that the world is fallen. However, this book offers a theological answer to social and human problems. On one hand, the book deals with the disappointing realities of life and highlights the personal, social, and moral failings that often characterize the human condition, and on the other hand, it points the way to new life, new realities, and new possibilities through the redemptive power of Jesus Christ. The book addresses many contemporary problems of life and endeavors to inspire and to instruct. The Bible says, "All scripture is given by inspiration of God, and is profitable for doctrine, for reproof, for correction, [and] for instruction" (II Timothy 3:16). In fact, the New Testament teaches that "God is love" and that God became a man in the person of Jesus Christ. The New Testament, in general, and the

Gospels, in particular, record Christ's message of hope and plan of salvation to those who believe in him.

The author and co-authors began writing this book many years ago. The sermons are different in style but are singular in how they attempt to illustrate biblical verses in meaningful ways by providing scholarly information, critical interpretations, and personal experiences. The sermons are meant for all audiences, regardless of race, gender, or denomination. Preaching is a tremendous task and the minister who undertakes such a major responsibility shares a message from his or her own knowledge, interpretations, and experiences. As such, the authors present these sermons from their own perspectives in a way that addresses the deepest need and aspirations of the human spirit. We agree with the twentieth century religious leader Howard Thurman, in his understanding of "worship," which "should not seek to undermine whatever may be the religious context which gives meaning and richness to your particular life, but rather to deepen the authentic lines along which your quest for spiritual reality has led you." Using resources from our individual religious context, we strive to achieve the same purpose.

In many church traditions, including the African American tradition, it is common for ministers to ask, "Can I get a witness?" These sermons are witnesses to the living presence of God in the world. One of the co-authors, Mrs. Annie Mae Nix, was not a licensed or ordained minister but she was a witness who thoroughly enjoyed sharing her testimony of God's goodness and grace to everyone, everywhere.

Hopefully, you will find strength and healing by reading about the goodness and grace of God, the love of Christ, and the inspiration of the Holy Spirit.

The Inspiration of the Holy Spirit

Putting First Things First

DR. ECHOL L. NIX, SR.

"But seek ye first the kingdom of God, and his righteousness; and all these things shall be added unto you." — St. Matthew 6:33

As a young boy in the first grade, I can recall learning the "Alphabet Song." We sang in order the twenty-six letters of the alphabet and added: "Now I've sang my ABCs, next time won't you sing with me." My teacher's objective in teaching this song was to show us how to put first things first. In junior high school, my English teacher would explain to the class the form of a friendly letter. She would often make us write letters in the following order: "heading," "salutation or greeting," "body," "complimentary close," and "personal signature." She would always make us put first things first. Even in college, my research professor taught us the principle of putting things first. For example, each research assignment had to be written in a certain order and in a certain way. In theses and dissertations, a general format is: Chapter 1—Introduction; Chapter 2—Review of Related Literature; Chapter 3—Design of the Investigation; Chapter 4—Analysis of the Data; Chapter 5—Summary, followed by the Conclusion, Recommendation, Bibliography, and Appendices. The objective was to put first things first.

One of the books I co-authored for the Alabama State Department of Education is titled *The Alabama Course of Study: Driver and Traffic Safety Education.* When writing the "pre-starting," "starting," "moving," "stopping," and "parking" procedures for a car, my objective was to put each procedure in order, according to the driver's purpose. In other words, I was trying to put first things first. This brings us to our text which was written by the Apostle Matthew. Matthew was his Greek name and he was also called Levi (which was his Hebrew name). He was a tax collector. In Hebrew, Matthew's name means "gift of the Lord." However, we know from his trade that he delighted himself in the "gift of others." He is given credit for authoring one book in the New Testament. His name is ascribed to his book. Out of the four gospels, the book of Matthew has the most chapters. Matthew consists of twenty-eight chapters, Mark consists of sixteen chapters, Luke consists of twenty-four chapters, and John consists of twenty-one chapters.

By thoroughly reading and studying the book, you will find that Matthew's Gospel is straight-forward. He writes: "But seek ye first the kingdom of God, and his righteousness; and all these things shall be added unto you." As I attempt to exegete the text, three things come to my mind. First, we must seek God. Second, we must seek His righteousness. Third, we must work and wait for our rewards.

Before we can seek God we need to know some things about God. The first chapter of Genesis gives us a bird's eye view of the power and goodness of God. Genesis 1:1–3 states: "In the beginning God created the heaven and the earth. And the earth was without form, and void; and darkness *was* upon the face of the deep. And the spirit of God moved upon the face of the waters. And God said, "Let there be light: and there was light." In the first chapter of Genesis, there is an emphasis on creation. God is the creator. In Chapter 1, God (called *Elohim*) is transcendent (separated from the material universe) and God is powerful (by speaking things into being). There is no struggle to bring order to chaos but God calls things into existence. Like the notes of a symphony, certain phrases appear and reappear; for example, "And God said," "God called (or named)," "God saw that it was good," "God made," "And there was evening, and there was morning." Hence, Genesis 1 is written in a poetic (or liturgical) style with repeated phrases for emphasis.

In addition to asking, "How can I know God?," a question could be: "How do I seek God?" God is spirit and they that worship Him must worship Him in Spirit and in Truth. Worship is one way to seek God. Through worship one can edify, glorify, sanctify, and magnify His Holy name. Worship has been defined as four attitudes that one should cultivate for the purpose of godliness: (1) It is a focusing on and responding to God. (2) It is done in spirit and in truth. (3) It is expected publicly and privately. (4) It is a spiritual discipline to be cultivated.

Nevertheless, in Matthew 16:16, Peter makes a bold statement which shows his recognition of Christ's divinity: "And Simon Peter answered and said, 'Thou art the Christ, the Son of the living God.'" In John 20:28, when the resurrected Jesus appears to Thomas and shows Thomas the scars in His hands and His side, Thomas worships with an immediate reply, "My Lord and my God." In Revelation 4:8, we are told that four creatures around the throne worship God day and night crying, without ceasing: "Holy, holy, holy Lord God Almighty, which was, and is, and is to come." Then in Revelation 4:11 the twenty-four elders around the throne of God in Heaven are said to have worshipped Him by casting their crowns at His feet, falling down before Him, and saying, "Thou art worthy, O Lord, to receive glory and honor and power: for thou hast created all things, and for thy pleasure they are and were created."

Nevertheless, prayer is another way to seek God and there is power in prayer. I have seen how the power of prayer can bring people who doctors had given up to die come back to good health and life. My wife, Annie Mae was given only six months to a year to live after her diagnosis. Doctors told her that multiple myeloma, a cancer of the plasma cells, would take her life in less than a year. I prayed, she prayed, other family members prayed, church members prayed, and friends prayed for her. It was by the grace of God that she lived an additional sixteen years. Every day was not easy but she held on to God's unchanging hand. She saw high mountains and deep valleys but she served God, testified and witnessed in His name, and praised Him for His goodness and His grace. In addition, I have seen how the power of prayer can bring convicted felons from the prison to the pulpit. Prayer has made saints out of sinners. The power of prayer delivered Paul and Silas out of the Philippian jail. God intervened for Paul and Silas in a miraculous way to the point that their jailer came to Christ. The jailer asked, "Sirs, what must I do to be saved? And they said, Believe on the Lord Jesus Christ, and thou shalt be saved, and thy house . . . And when he had brought them into his house, he set meat before them, and rejoiced, believing in God with all his house" (Acts 16:30–31, 34). The power of prayer opened Hannah's barren womb. She had a son who became a priest, a prophet, and a judge. His name was Samuel.

Furthermore, studying the Bible is another way to seek God. The "Word" in Greek is *Logos*. John 1:1 states, "In the beginning was the Word, and the Word was with God, and the Word was God." Psalms 119:105 states, "Thy word *is* a lamp unto my feet, and light unto my path." Paul told Timothy in II Timothy 2:15, "Study to shew thyself approved unto God, a workman that needeth not to be ashamed, rightly dividing the word of truth." Dr. J. Vernon McGee recommends seven steps in studying the Bible: (1) Begin with prayer, (2) Read the Bible, (3) Study the Bible, (4) Meditate upon the Bible, (5) Read what others have written on the Bible, (6) Obey the Bible, and (7) Pass it on to others. An unknown author expresses it this way: "The Bible—Know it in your head; Store it in your heart; Show it in your life, Sow it in the world." I highly recommend for you not to just read the Bible good but read it *real* good. In his poem "When You Read the Bible Through," Amos Wells writes:

> I supposed I knew my Bible, reading piecemeal hit or miss, Now a bit of John or Matthew, now a snatch of Genesis, certain chapters of Isaiah, certain Psalms (the Twenty-third!): Twelfth of Romans, first of Proverbs— yes, I thought I knew the Word! But I found that thorough reading was a different thing to do, And the way was unfamiliar, When I read the Bible through. Oh, the massive mighty volume! Oh the treasures manifold! Oh, the beauty and the wisdom and the grace it proved to hold! As the story of the Hebrews swept in majesty along, As it leaped in waves prophetic; as it burst to sacred song. As it gleamed with Christly omens, The Old Testament was new, Strong with cumulative power, When I read the Bible through.

Oh, imperial Jeremiah, with his keen witty mind! And the blunt old Nehemiah, and Ezekial refined! Newly came the Minor Prophets, each with his distinctive robes; Newly came the song idyllic, and the tragedy of Job; Deuteronomy, the regal, To a towering mountain grew With its comrade peaks around it, When I read the Bible through.

What a radiant procession as the pages rise and fall! James the sturdy, John the tender—oh, the myriad-minded Paul! Vast apocalyptic glories wheel and thunder, flash and flame, While the church Triumphant raises one Incomparable Name. Ah, the story of the Saviour, Never glows supremely true, till you read it whole and swiftly, till you read the Bible through!

Second, as we seek God, we must seek His righteousness. The Apostle Paul was on target when he stated, "Brethren, my heart's desire and prayer to God for Israel is, that they might be saved. For I bear them record that they have a zeal of God but not according to knowledge. For they being ignorant of God's righteousness, and going about to establish their own righteousness, have not submitted themselves unto the righteousness of God (Romans 10:1–3). King Solomon could not have stated it any better in Proverbs 3:5–6, "Trust in the Lord with all thine heart; and lean not unto thine own understanding. In all thy ways acknowledge Him; and he shall direct thy paths." It behooves us to remember what Jesus says in Matthew 5:20: "For I say unto you, That except your righteousness shall exceed *the righteousness* of the scribes and Pharisees, ye shall in no case enter into the kingdom of heaven." It is highly mandatory, necessary, and essential that we seek His righteousness.

To obtain God's righteousness, one must be born again. Jesus informs us in Saint John 3:3, "Except a man be born again, he cannot see the kingdom of God." In order to obtain God's righteousness, one must have a pure heart. Matthew 5:8 says, "Blessed *are* the pure in heart, for they shall see God." Also, in order to obtain God's righteousness, one must have meekness and not weakness. Jesus says in Matthew 5:5, "Blessed *are* the meek: for they shall inherit the earth."

Nevertheless, a final point is to work and wait on your rewards. According to the Bible, there will be different levels of rewards in heaven. Our rewards in heaven will be based upon our work here on earth. One of the rewards is found in I Thessalonians 2:19, the "Crown of Rejoicing." This crown is given to the ones who served as a witness for Christ while ministering to others. Another reward is called the "Crown of Righteousness." Paul alludes to this crown in II Timothy 4:6–8 as he nears his death. He stated, "For I am now ready to be offered, and the time of *my* departure is at hand. I have fought a good fight, I have finished *my* course, I have kept the faith: Henceforth there is laid up for *me* a crown of righteousness, which the Lord, the righteous judge, shall give *me* at that day: and not to *me* only, but unto all them also that love his appearing." This crown will be given to the ones who were faithful in the Lord all the way to the end. Personally, I would like to hear from Christ, "Servant of God, well done."

Another reward that will be given is the "Crown of Life." James 1:12 alludes to this crown: "Blessed is the man that endureth temptation: for when he is tried, he shall receive the crown of life, which the Lord hath promised to them that love him." This crown will be given to the ones who endured the test of trials and temptations. Testing will either drive a person to the Lord or away from the Lord. I would like to think that Job and others who suffered would receive this crown. Personally, I am a witness that trials and tribulations can produce a closer relationship with Christ. Someone has expressed it in the following way:

> Is there no other way open, God,
> Except through sorrow, pain, and loss,
> To stamp Christ's likeness on my soul—
> No other way except the Cross?
> And then a voice stills all my soul
> As stilled the waves of Galilee,
> "Can't thou not bear the furnace heat
> If midst the flames I walk with thee?
> I bore the cross. I know its weight.
> I drank the cup I hold for thee.
> Can'st thou not follow where I lead?

I'll give thee strength. Lean hard on me."

The last reward that I am going to talk about is the "Crown of Glory." This crown is found in I Peter 5:4, "And when the chief Shepherd shall appear, ye shall receive a crown of glory that fadeth not away." Glory has size and shape. The Psalmist says: "The heavens declare the glory of God; and the firmament sheweth his handywork" (Psalms 19:1). I am under the impression that the Crown of Glory is wonderful and worth waiting for. Eventually, we can expect to share in this glory. The songwriter expressed his or her expectation in a personal and traditional way:

GLORY, GLORY, HALLELUJAH!

> Glory, glory, hallelujah!
> Since I laid my burdens down
>
> I feel better, so much better
> Since I laid my burdens down
>
> Friends don't treat me like they used to
> Since I laid my burdens down
>
> Feel like shouting "Hallelujah!"
> Since I laid my burdens down
>
> Burdens down, Lord, burdens down Lord
> Since I laid my burdens down

I am climbing Jacob's ladder
Since I laid my burden down

Ev'ry round goes higher and higher
Since I laid my burdens down

I'm goin' home to live with Jesus
Since I laid my burdens down.

Again, seek God, seek His Righteousness, and work and wait on your rewards. In other words, while traveling along your spiritual journey, practice "Putting First Things First."

It is Coming Up Again

Dr. Echol L. Nix, Sr.

*"Be not deceived; God is not mocked; for what-
soever a man soweth, that shall he also reap."*
— Galatians 6:7

I remember so vividly growing up as a young boy in Montevallo, Alabama. In the spring, my father would borrow Uncle Fred Caddell's mule named Georgia. Georgia was used for plowing the fields of families and friends in the community. After my father completed the task of plowing the field, my mother would go to the seed store and buy seeds to plant crops such as watermelons, squash, corn, peas, and okra. It was baffling to understand how a very small seed could be planted in the ground and in a week or two weeks sprout up as a plant. I could not understand how that little seed could grow to be tall and large. I did not know anything about the process of germination, but I knew the seeds went down and came back up. In addition to crops germinating from the environment, I was also confused about the process of human conception. How could a little baby start out so small and become so big? Then, it occurred to me that whatever we plant will come up again. Some practical wisdom through the ages and some traditional aphorisms are relevant here: "What is done in the dark will come to the light," "What goes around, will come back around," "You reap what you sow," and "What goes up, will come down."

In other words, whatever we plant, whether right or wrong, good or bad, will come up again. Because of this reality, I would like to highlight two points: (1) eliminate bad seeds and (2) plant good seeds.

The first seed that should be eliminated is the seed of hatred. Hatred is a form of dislike. It is a seed that has caused men, women, boys, and girls to kill each other without a cause. Much of the violence in our country—past and present—results from hatred. The disease of hatred lingers and has dangerous consequences. Hatred is not restricted to a particular ethnic people, social class or religious denomination. This seed has been planted and rooted across the human spectrum and affects everyone. According to Dr. Martin Luther King, Jr., "Hatred paralyzes life, confuses life, and darkens life."

It is my great hope that the seed of hatred would be eradicated, eliminated, and terminated. Edwin Markham once stated, "There is a destiny that makes us brothers; none goes his way alone. All that we send into the lives of others comes back into our own." The seed of hatred caused Esau to hate his brother Jacob for many years. Genesis 27:41 states: "And Esau hated Jacob because of the blessing wherewith his father blessed him: and Esau said in his heart, The days of mourning for my father are at hand; then will I slay [kill] my brother Jacob." Many times people will hate you just because you are you. Dr. Martin Luther King, Jr. also stated, "We must live together as brothers and sisters or perish together as fools."

The next seed that should be eliminated is the seed of jealousy. Jealousy is a feeling that can result in terrible acts, committed overtly or covertly, against someone. Covetousness is a form of jealousy. Exodus 20:17 states: "Thou shalt not covet thy neighbour's house, thou shalt not covet thy neighbour's wife, nor his manservant, nor his maidservant, nor his ox, nor his ass, nor any thing that is thy neighbour's." The first murder in the Bible took place because of jealousy. Cain killed his brother Abel (Genesis 4:8). Because of jealousy, Joseph was sold to the Ishmaelites for twenty pieces of silver (Genesis 37:28). Take a look at what jealousy did to King Saul in I Samuel 18:6–12:

> And it came to pass as they came, when David was returned from the slaughter of the Philistine, that the women came out of all cities of Israel, singing and dancing to meet King Saul, with tambourines, with joy, and with instruments of music. And the women answered one another as they played, and said, Saul hath slain

his thousands, and David his ten thousands. And Saul was very wroth, and the saying displeased him; and he said, They have ascribed unto David ten thousands, and to me they have ascribed but thousands: and what can he have more but the kingdom? And Saul eyed David from that day and forward. And it came to pass on the morrow, that the evil spirit from God came upon Saul, and he prophesied in the midst of the house: and David played with his hand, as at other times: and there was a javelin in Saul's hand. And Saul cast the javelin; for he said, I will smite David even to the wall with it. And David avoided out of his presence twice. And Saul was afraid of David, because the Lord was with him, and was departed from Saul.

Unfortunately and regrettably, jealousy can occur among family members, friends, and church members. Church members? Yes! Jealousy can infiltrate a church family, especially when the "Tate family" is part of the church. The names of the Tate family members are: 1) Daddy DevasTate 2) Mama DicTate 3) Sister AgiTate 4) Brother HesiTate 5) Cousin Procrastinate and 6) Niece or Nephew Fabricate. Please note that some of the above family members can be found in every church and household.

The next seed that should be eliminated is the seed of disobedience which is the refusal or failure to obey. My mother is gone to be with the Lord; however, she once told me in plain speech that "a hard head would make a soft tail." At that time, I did not know what she meant, but I have a better understanding now. We have too many people young and old alike who do not adhere to sound instruction and discipline. Many don't even listen to or consider alternative thoughts and actions but are so wrapped up (and tangled up) in doing their own thing. According to Pastor Johnny Carter, a minister in Montgomery, Alabama: "A fool will get lost and then ask for directions but a wise man asks for directions before getting lost." Disobedience caused Adam and Eve to be put out of the Garden of Eden (Genesis 3:23). It caused the Israelites to wander in the wilderness for forty years (Numbers 14:29–34). As young people travel along life's highway, it's important to listen to parents who have traveled the same road or from others who have had similar experiences. In the "Decalogue," which is another name for the Ten Commandments, it says: "Honor thy father and thy mother: that thy days may be long upon the land which the Lord thy God giveth thee" (Exodus 20:12).

Humility is being able to examine oneself before you are able to live with oneself. The last piece of advice that Polonius gives his son Laertes in Shakespeare's *Hamlet* is: "To thine own self be true, And it must follow, as the night the day, Thou canst not then be false to any man." St. Luke 14:11 says, "For whosoever exalteth himself shall be abased; and he that humbleth himself shall be exalted." I often remember the words of my grandmother,

Mrs. Pearlie Nix, who was a wonderful Christian lady and who inspired many people. She shared her wisdom and experiences during my return visits from college at Mississippi Valley State University and once remarked: "No matter how high you go or how low you fall, never forget God." She knew that I would need God whether I graduated from college or not, became rich or poor, achieved success and fame or failed. She knew that the controlling factor in my life needed to be God. It is my goal to pass this advice on to others—young and old.

The next seed that needs to be terminated is the seed of lying. According to various lexicographers, "lying" is a false statement presented as being true. A lie is easy for an unsaved person to tell but should be difficult for a saved person to tell. The seed of lying has terrible consequences. For example, it has caused many innocent bystanders to be put on death row. It has freed many criminals who should have been incarcerated. It has caused husbands and wives, boyfriends and girlfriends to hurt each other physically, mentally, socially, emotionally, and spiritually. The seed of lying manifests itself in the White House, state house, courthouse, schoolhouse, church house, and in many personal houses. It does not discriminate on the basis of race, color, creed, gender, or age. It is found in all walks of life with all walks of people.

The first lie in the Bible started in Genesis 3:4 "And the serpent said unto the woman, Ye shall not surely die." Adam and Eve did not die physically the day that they ate the fruit. However, they died spiritually the moment they ate of the forbidden fruit. They were separated from God. Death is a form of separation. For this world to be better for all of us, we must stop lying. We must teach our spouses, children, and grandchildren not to lie. Lies can plague families and nations for generations to come. One lie leads to another. Exodus 20:16 states: "Thou shalt not bear false witness against thy neighbor." There are many other places for documentation on this point and one reference is Proverbs 12:22: "Lying lips are an abomination to the Lord: but they that deal truly are his delight."

Further, excessive alcohol and the accompanying disease of alcoholism need to be eliminated. People of all ages, races and places are affected by this seed. Alcohol comes in a variety of forms including beer, wine, whiskey, gin, vodka, rum, brandy, tequila, and others. The more alcohol that enters the bloodstream, the more the portions of the brain that control physical reflexes and coordination become depressed.[1] Alcohol's paralyzing and numbing effect on the brain begins at the higher center (cerebrum) and moves toward the lower center (medulla) of activity, as the concentration of alcohol in the bloodstream increases. The parts of the brain are affected in reverse order of their development. First the fore lobes (cerebrum) of the brain are affected; resulting in decreased

---

1   *Alliance for Safe Driving, License to Drive in Alabama.* New York: Delmar, 2000. 417.

ability to reason and make judgments, weakened social inhibitions, and changed attitude toward others. As the concentration increases, more of the forebrain is affected. In addition, alcohol reaches the cerebellum which controls sensory motor functions. The result is emotional instability, slow verbal responses, impaired vision, and a lack of coordination. At higher levels of concentration, the person is unable to stand or walk and can possibly lose consciousness. Death results when all of the brain, the upper spinal column, and the respiratory and heart control centers are anesthetized.[2]

In addition to the physical, mental, social, and emotional effects of alcoholism, there is also a spiritual effect. The Bible cautions against the abuse of alcohol. Proverbs 20:1 states, "Wine is a mocker, strong drink is raging: and whosoever is deceived thereby is not wise." St. Luke 21:34 alludes to the fact that drunkenness will cause a person not to be ready for the Lord's return. Habakkuk 2:15–16 warns that drinking leads to woe and shame. I Corinthians 6:10 points out that drunkards will not inherit the Kingdom of God.

The next seed that should not be planted is fornicating or pre-marital sex. The biological and spiritual effects of pre-marital sex are serious and just as important today as ever. Studies indicate that more than half of unmarried boys and nearly half of unmarried girls in America have

---

2   A *Basic Curriculum Guide for Teachers of Driver Education*. Alabama: Alabama State Dept. of Education, 2003. 72–73.

had sexual intercourse by the age of nineteen.[3] Pre-marital sex does not always encompass or maintain the desirable elements of fidelity, communication, trust, honesty, and sacrifice. It is usually based on physical attractiveness and infatuation which invariably results from a blind sentimentality without regard for true knowledge. The possibility of sexually transmitted diseases and the unexpected consequences of emotional distress and unwanted teenage pregnancies should be considered.

Choices bring consequences and consequences are sometimes overlooked. Life is a gift from God, regardless, but parenthood involves accountability, acceptability, and responsibility. Young people and old alike should be taught that reproduction is not the only criterion for manhood or womanhood. Without channeling feelings and controlling one's hormones, moments of pleasure can and often lead to a life of pain and shame. The Apostle Paul states: "Flee fornication. Every sin that a man doeth is without the body; but he that committeth fornication sinneth against his own body. What? know ye not that your body is the temple of the Holy Ghost which is in you, which ye have of God, and ye are not your own? For ye are bought with a price: therefore glorify God in your body, and in your spirit, which are God's" (1 Corinthians 6:18–20). Paul also states in 1 Thessalonians 4:3–4: "For this is the will of God, even your sanctification, that ye should abstain from fornication: That every one of you

---

3 Dye, J. "Sex." *The World Book Encyclopedia*. 1988.

should know how to possess his vessel in sanctification and honor." The church's position, based on the Bible, should be abstinence until marriage.

Connected to fornication is adultery (or extra-marital sex), and the Bible condemns adultery. Under the Mosaic Law, adultery was punishable by death. Leviticus 20:10 states: "And the man that committeth adultery with another man's wife, even he that committeth adultery with his neighbor's wife, the adulterer and the adulteress shall surely be put to death." Adultery has caused many men, women, boys, and girls to be put in dangerous and deadly situations. It has caused the deterioration and termination of many marriages. It has caused families, friends, and children to suffer unnecessarily.

I am reminded of a story, borrowed from the Reverend Jesse Jackson. The story goes: A young man told his father that he would like to talk with him. The father said, "What do you want to talk about son?" The son said, "I want to talk to you about marrying Keisha." The father said, "I'm sorry son, but you cannot marry Keisha because Keisha is your sister but your mother doesn't know it." Then the son said, "Well, I would like to marry Karen." The father sighed and said, "Again, you cannot marry Karen because Karen is your sister but your mother doesn't know it." Frustrated, the son finally said, "Well then, I would like to marry Kathy." The father took a breath and replied, "Son, you cannot marry Kathy either because Kathy is your sister but your mother doesn't know it."

So the young man was both disappointed and confused. He then went to his mother and said, "Mother I would like to talk to you." She said, "Son, what would you like to talk to me about?" He said, "I told Daddy I would like to marry Keisha, Karen, and Kathy, but he said that they are my sisters and you don't know it." The mother hesitated for a moment and said, "Well, son, that's not your daddy but he doesn't know it." Stories like this can bring pain and suffering as well as a complete surprise.

Adultery caused King David and his entire family to suffer. The prophet Nathan told King David these words from the Lord:

> Wherefore hast thou despised the commandment of the Lord, to do evil in his sight? Thou hast killed Uriah the Hittite with the sword, and hast taken his wife to be thy wife, and hast slain him with the sword of the children of Ammon. Now therefore the sword shall never depart from thine house; because thou hast despised me, and hast taken the wife of Uriah the Hittite to be thy wife. Thus saith the Lord, Behold, I will raise up evil against thee out of thine own house, and I will take thy wives before thine eyes, and give them unto thy neighbor, and he shall lie with thy wives in the sight of this sun. For thou didst it secretly: but I will do this thing before all Israel, and before the sun (II Samuel 12:9–12).

The seed of adultery will never be pleasing in the eyesight

of God. I highly recommend it to be eradicated, eliminated, and terminated. It could bring openness to what we thought was a secret.

My next point is to plant good seeds. The first seed I would recommend to be planted is the seed of righteousness. Jesus said in Matthew 6:33, "But seek ye first the kingdom of God, and his righteousness; and all these things shall be added unto you." Righteousness is a state of being morally and spiritually upright. Our lifestyle should be an archetype of the Bible. To be a Christian, Jesus must be our example. We have too many people educated and uneducated who believe that they can do anything in the eyesight of God and still be a Christian. This is wrongful thinking. According to the Bible, a tree is known by the fruit it bears. So, a Christian will bear good fruit. The seed of righteousness will enable one to demonstrate qualities such as integrity, truthfulness, honesty and goodness. Good seeds must be planted in the minds of boys, girls, men, and women of all races and places. Although there is no guaranteed results with raising children, exposing them to good examples and role models can make a crucial difference. Parents, grandparents, and guardians should do the best they can and train children up in the way they should go and (hopefully) when the child is older, he or she will not depart from it (Proverbs 22:6).

The next seed that should be planted is the seed of education. Education is often defined as a process of knowledge gained through teaching and learning.

Personally, I have found education to be a continuous process which starts before birth and ends at death. A good biblical and secular education foundation should be incorporated in each person's life. According to the Bible, "the fear of the Lord is the beginning of knowledge: but fools despise wisdom and instruction." Again, I feel that education without salvation will bring destruction. President Theodore Roosevelt wrote: "To educate a person in mind and not in morals is to educate a menace to society." Dr. Martin Luther King, Jr. further stated: "Intelligence plus character is the goal of a true education."

The next seed that needs to be planted is that of perseverance. Perseverance is the ability to press on and to not give up. It means being persistent and being determined to go all the way to the end. Too many people give up and give out before even starting. Many stay on "Easy Street" and "Rest Boulevard." An unknown author stated, "It's not how big the dog in the fight but how much fight is in the dog." Faith is a key factor in maintaining perseverance. Faith is believing that you can when others say that you can't. Hebrews 11:1 says, "Now faith is the substance of things hoped for, the evidence of things not seen."

Patience is another seed that needs to be planted. It is the ability to execute calmness, self-control, and the willingness to tolerate delay. It is being able to humble oneself to wait. Isaiah 40:31 informs, "But they that wait upon the Lord shall renew their strength; they shall mount up with wings as eagles; they shall run, and not be weary;

and they shall walk, and not faint." Patience can bring out the best in us. However, impatience can bring out the worst in us. Remember to plant the seed of patience.

As I close, the last seed I recommend for planting is the seed of love. According to the Greek language, there are three kinds of love. The first is *agape*, meaning "Godly love." The second is called *phileo*, meaning "brotherly love." The third is *eros*, meaning "sexual love" or "an intimate affection between two or more parties." "Godly love" is my final point.

Agape love is the strongest of all. It represents God's love for all creation. The love of God is demonstrated through the death and resurrection of Jesus Christ. St. John 3:16 states: "For God so loved the world that he gave his only begotten Son, that whosoever believeth in him shall not perish but have everlasting life." Just as God so loved the world, we should also plant seeds of love everywhere. We must plant them in every church house and schoolhouse, in the White House, in state houses (and in all other houses!). They must be planted in every state and nation. Let it be known that the greatest of all is love (I Corinthians 13). The words of James Rowe come to mind:

I was sinking deep in sin, far from the peaceful shore.
Very deeply stained within, sinking to rise no more;
But the Master of the sea heard my despairing cry,
From the waters lifted me, now safe am I.

Love lifted me!

Love lifted me! When nothing else could help,

Love lifted me!

All my heart to Him I'll give, ever to Him I'll cling,

In His blessed presence live, ever His praises sing.

Love so mighty and so true merits my soul's best
songs;

Faithful, loving service, too, to Him belongs.

Love lifted me!

Love lifted me! When nothing else could help,

Love lifted me!

Put Your Trust in God

Dr. Echol L. Nix, Sr.

"Trust in the Lord with all thine heart and lean not unto thine own understanding: In all thy ways acknowledge Him, and He shall direct thy paths."
— Proverbs 3:5–6

The book of Proverbs is a part of Wisdom literature and is considered a poetry book. Job, Psalms, Proverbs, Ecclesiastes, and the Song of Solomon are also in this category. Proverbs consists of sayings, commandments and long poems. Certain themes are honesty, diligence, trustworthiness, the cultivation of true and proper speech, the correct attitudes towards wealth and poverty, and moral values. Most biblical scholars agree that Solomon was the author of Proverbs, Ecclesiastes, and the Song of Solomon. Solomon is considered the wisest man that ever lived. God granted him this wisdom while still a child. He wrote 3,000 proverbs and 1,005 songs. Solomon was the first king to build God's temple, which was the first temple. It was built in

Jerusalem around 950 B.C.E. The Queen of Sheba heard of the fame of Solomon and came from the Far East to see for herself and to ask him hard questions. Solomon answered all of her questions. She replied, "Behold the half was not told: your wisdom and prosperity surpass the fame which I heard" (I Kings 10:1–10).

If you read I Kings, chapter eleven, you will find that Solomon did not always demonstrate the wisdom God granted him. Solomon married many women, perhaps to foster better relationships with neighboring countries. Solomon, reportedly, had seven hundred wives and three hundred concubines. "For it came to pass when Solomon was old, that his wives turned away his heart after other gods; and his heart was not perfect with the Lord his God, as was the heart of David his father" (I Kings 11:4).

Nevertheless, it is sad that we have in our society men, women, boys, and girls who have also turned their minds and hearts away from serving God. Solomon started serving idol gods such as Chemosh, Molech, and Milcom. As a way forward and as a way of correcting this problem, I will discuss four points. (1) Trust in the Lord with all thine heart, (2) Lean not to thy own understanding, (3) In all thy ways acknowledge Him, and (4) He shall direct thy paths.

Let us look at point one: (1) Trust in the Lord with all thine heart. According to *Webster's Dictionary*, the word "trust" means to have "confidence," "to depend on," or "to believe in." Personally, trust means "to put your weight on God." Many of you may watch or have seen championship wrestling on television or in person. Some of the heavyweight wrestlers about my size would body slam and jump on top of a wrestler with all of their weight. That is what we should do—put all of our weight on God. A songwriter once said, "Take your burdens to the Lord and leave them there." Too many people put their trust in friends and family. Friends and family may have good intentions and mean well, but they may not always prove reliable or trustworthy when needed or requested. All of these people can fool you, deceive you, and destroy you. Friends can praise you one day and unfairly criticize you the next day. Family members can be related to you by blood but it's not always possible to depend on them when the going gets tough. Many put their total trust in palm readers, lottery tickets and other forms of gambling but these are rather uncertain deities. Some put trust in stock markets only to see fluctuations in the market, sometimes producing an economic recession or depression.

Moreover, King Solomon was able to write the book of Proverbs. He had seen everything under the sun, which he called "vanity and vexation of spirit." He studied science, the laws of nature, human and social phenomena, and philosophy. However, he found a void and an emptiness without God. Solomon would agree with Lord Alfred Tennyson who wrote: "Our little systems have their day; They have their day and cease to be: They are but broken lights of thee, But thou, O Lord, art more than they."

Whether we are starting college, a new job, marriage, buying a home, or getting ready to venture out on one's own for the first time, it behooves all of us to remember that our trust must be in God. Personally, I have found Him to be a way-maker and a problem-solver. The Hebrew boys experienced Him in a hot, fiery furnace. Daniel experienced Him in a lion's den. Elijah experienced Him on Mount Carmel.

As a country boy from Montevallo, Alabama, I did not understand what the choir meant when they sang, "The Lord will make a way somehow." After losing my mother in 1985, my sister in 1986, my father in 1987, personally suffering serious heart and blood pressure problems, pastoring from 1985–1990, caring for my wife—who was given eight to ten months to live due to a cancer diagnosis but who survived another sixteen years, which made her a cornerstone in medical research—I have come to learn what it truly means to trust in God. God brought me from plowing my uncle's mule all the way through graduate school. He brought me from the wrong side of the track to the right side of the track. I was lost and drifting along life's highway with no direction or guidance. I was a walking dead man—too dead to be alive and too alive to be dead. God took my sins and washed them away in the blood of Jesus. Augustine wrote in his *Confessions*, "Humans are restless until we rest in God." Since accepting my call to the Christian ministry on April 1, 1984, I have a greater peace and satisfaction. My testimony is the same as the one who said: "What a wonderful change in my life has been wrought, Since Jesus came into my heart; I have light in my soul for which long I had sought, Since Jesus came into my heart."

Second, Solomon says, "Lean not to thine own understanding." "Thine own understanding" is making self your priority. Self can easily become "selfish" and is in close company with me, my, myself and I. It can make you think that you are right and everybody else is wrong. "Thine own understanding" can turn your dignity into misery and it can turn your hopes into despair. It can turn your gladness into sadness, your success into failures. When I think about self, I often think about the poem "Man in the Glass" written by Peter Winbrow:

When you get what you want in your struggle for self
And the world makes you king for a day,
Just go to the mirror and look at yourself
And see what that man has to say.

For it isn't your father or mother or wife
Whose judgment upon you must pass.
The fellow whose verdict counts most in your life
Is the one staring back from the glass.

You may be like Jack Horner and chisel a plum
And think you're a wonderful guy.
But the man in the glass says you're only a bum

If you can't look him straight in the eye.

He's the fellow to please–never mind all the rest,
For he's with you clear to the end.
And you've passed your most dangerous, difficult test
If the man in the glass is your friend.

You may fool the whole world down the pathway of years,
    And get pats on the back as you pass.
But your final reward will be heartache and tears
    If you've cheated the man in the glass.

Third, Solomon says "In all ways acknowledge Him."
"Acknowledge Him" means to give God the proper respect
and honor. In the book of Numbers, Moses and Aaron
did not give God the proper respect and honor. It cost
both of them dearly. They were not permitted to enter
the Promised Land with Joshua and Caleb. God had to
give their jobs to Joshua and Eleazar.

We must never forget to acknowledge God in all
of our ways. Some acknowledge Him as "El Shaddai,"
meaning "God Almighty." Others acknowledge Him as
"Jehovah Jireh," "the Lord will provide." He has also been
called "Jehovah Nissi," "the Lord is our Banner." My wife
often called Him "Jehovah Rapha," "the Lord that heals."
Moses acknowledged Him in the book of Genesis when
he supposedly wrote: "In the beginning God created the
Heavens and the earth." Joshua acknowledged Him when

he said, "As for me and my house, we will serve the Lord." David acknowledged Him when he stated, "The Lord is my shepherd, I shall not want." Job acknowledged Him by saying, "the Lord gave and the Lord taketh away, blessed it to be the name of the Lord." The seraphims in Isaiah 6 acknowledged Him by saying, "Holy, Holy, Holy, the Lord of hosts; the whole earth is full of His glory." So again: (1) Trust in the Lord with all thine heart, (2) Lean not to thy own understanding, and (3) In all thy ways acknowledge Him. The last point is: (4) He shall direct thy paths.

As you embark on a higher plane, your paths must be directed by God. For our paths to be directed by God, our total trust must be put in God. God directed the path of Adam, but Adam did not totally trust God. The results of his disobedience brought sin to humankind.

God directed the path of Noah to build an ark. Many people thought he was crazy. God was getting Noah ready for the raindrops ahead. Also, in Genesis 12, God told Abraham to leave his hometown and go to a land that God would show him. The land God showed Abraham was Canaan, often called the Promised Land.

God directed Moses to be a great leader, deliverer, and lawgiver. In the case of Moses, read Exodus 3, especially verses 13–15. In Genesis chapters 37–50, God directs the path of Joseph, bringing him from a pit to a palace by elevating him to the position of a governor in Egypt. God's direction is also revealed through the forty or more men who were inspired to write the Bible. Many years later, the

Bible was divided up into various categories such as:

The Books of the Old Testament

Law Books or Pentateuch

Genesis, Exodus, Leviticus, Numbers, Deuteronomy

History Books

Joshua, Judges, Ruth, I Samuel, II Samuel, I Kings, II Kings, I Chronicles, II Chronicles, Ezra, Nehemiah, Esther

Books of Poetry

Job, Psalms, Proverbs, Ecclesiastes, Song of Solomon

Major Prophets and Prophecies

Isaiah, Jeremiah, Lamentations, Ezekiel, Daniel

Minor Prophets and Prophecies

Hosea, Joel, Amos, Obediah, Jonah, Micah, Nahum, Habakkuk, Zephaniah, Haggai, Zechariah, Malachi

The Books of the New Testament

Gospels

Matthew, Mark, Luke, John

SYNOPTIC GOSPELS

Matthew, Mark, Luke

HISTORY

Acts

LETTERS OR EPISTLES WRITTEN BY PAUL

Romans, I Corinthians, II Corinthians, Galatians, Ephesians, Philippians, Colossians, I Thessalonians, II Thessalonians, I Timothy, II Timothy, Titus, Philemon, Hebrews

PASTORAL EPISTLES

I Timothy, II Timothy, Titus

PRISON EPISTLES

Ephesians, Philippians, Colossians, Philemon

THE GENERAL EPISTLES

James, I Peter, II Peter, I John, II John, III John, Jude

THE BOOK OF PROPHECY

Revelation

Finally, God directed the path of Jesus. He was anointed and appointed to be the Savior of the world. He stated: "For I have come to seek and to save that which was lost" (St. Luke 19:10).

He was both human and divine. He was in the beginning before the beginning had ever begun to begin. On His mother's side He was in time, but on His Father's side He was before time. He is the only one whom I know who held his mother before His mother held Him. On His mother's side, He prayed to the Father, but on His Father's side He answered and answers countless prayers. On His mother's side, He was tempted, but on His Father's side, He lived without sin. On His mother's side, He had to learn, but on His Father's side, He created wisdom, knowledge, and understanding.

To the architect, He is the chief cornerstone. To the banker, He is the hidden treasure. To the Christian, He is the Son of God and the Savior of the world. To the doctor, He is the great physician. To the educator, He is a teacher's lesson plan. To the florist, he is the Rose of Sharon and the Lilly of the Valley. To the geologist, he is the Rock of Ages. To the juror, He is a true witness. To the news broadcaster, he brings tidings of great joy. To the ophthalmologist, He is the Light of the world. To the philanthropist, he is the gift of love. To the student, He is the master teacher.

To the theologian, He is the author and finisher of Christian faith. To the sinner, He is the Lamb of God who takes away the sins of the world.

Tell the world He died, but He didn't stay dead. He rose with all power—not black power or white power, not Alabama power or Georgia power, not wind power or solar power, not electric power or hydraulic power—

but all power in His hands. Tell the world about Jesus, tell about His love, tell about His grace, tell about His power . . .

Dare to be Different

Dr. Echol L. Nix, Jr.

"And be not conformed to this world: but be ye transformed by the renewing of your mind, that ye may prove what is that good, and acceptable, and perfect will of God." — Romans 12:2

The above text is from the *King James Version*. The *Oxford Study Bible* says: "Conform no longer to the pattern of this present world, but be transformed by the renewing of your minds." *The New Living Translation* says: "Don't copy the behavior and customs of this world, but let God transform you into a new person by changing the way you think. Then you will know what God wants you to do, and you will know how good and pleasing and perfect his will really is." However, *my* version would begin: "Dare to be different . . ." In all of these versions, the Apostle Paul's basic message condemns conformity. *Webster's Collegiate Dictionary* defines "conformity" as "compliance or acquiescence to prevailing social standards, attitudes, or practices." This is precisely what Paul is discouraging. Paraphrases of his admonition could include: "Do not be another common or average person, but be a cut above the rest." "Do not adopt a philosophy based on the latest and most popular opinion poll, but make personal decisions based on critical conceptions of what is true and beautiful and good." "Do not be easily persuaded by the majority for the sake of doing business as usual but have a moral conscience and take a stand on issues that challenge the status quo."

Paul admonishes the early Christians in Rome to be counter-culture or non-conformists. He challenges them to "be different." Paul's command contains two parts. First of all, he says, "And be not conformed to this world." Second, he tells "how" not to conform to this world. So the two parts are "be not" and "how not." The "how not" is by renewing your mind or having an inner experience of faith and love. In the New Testament, especially in John chapter 3, Jesus calls this a "new birth"—being "born again" or "born from above." The new birth results in new thoughts which produce different habits and a change in one's character. In verse 2, Paul is clear in his command against conformity. However, his command is incomplete. He says, "*Be not* conformed" and he tells us "*how not* to conform" but he doesn't say "*why not* conform." We can ask Paul: "Why not imitate the ways of the world? After all, we live in the world, so why not be 'of the world?'" We are associated with the world, with our families, friendships, organizations (such as fraternities, sororities and voluntary associations), political parties, economic, social, and educational groups, and banking and financial institutions, among others. This is the world and there are conscious and un-conscious influences on our thoughts and actions through sales and advertisements, media programs, propaganda, radio and television commercials, contemporary music, images of success and recognition. These are only a few ways that we experience the world. We live in the world and we are intimately involved and inextricably connected with the world, so *why not* conform to this world?

Unfortunately, Paul does not answer, but we can assume that he thought there are fundamental flaws with this world. This world is flawed by sin, evil, religious and social division, pride, terrorism, racism, sexism (and many other -isms!). For every historical period of peace and tranquility, there have been counterperiods of war and violence. Empathy and compassion are matched with hatred and unforgiveness. Human achievement and intelligence are coupled with injustices and ignorance. The eighteenth century philosopher, Jean Jacques Rousseau was convinced that humanity is essentially good, but that its original nature has been corrupted by society. Another eighteenth century philosopher, Immanuel Kant, disagreed with Rousseau and argued that humanity has a natural inclination to do evil. Kant follows the early church theologian, St. Augustine, who shared the view of a natural human tendency to do evil. Perhaps

Augustine was influenced by the Apostle Paul's confession in Romans 7:18–19: "For I know that nothing good dwells within me, that is, in my flesh. I can will what is right, but I cannot do it. For I do not do the good I want, but the evil I do not want is what I do. Now if I do what I do not want, it is no longer I that do it, but sin which dwells within me."

The question then becomes how to overcome this tendency. Paul goes further to write: "O wretched man that I am! Who shall deliver me from the body of death? I thank God through Jesus Christ our Lord" (Romans 7:24–25a). Therefore, religion and ethics become necessary to transform the inherent flaws in the world. For Paul, the "corrupted" is entangled with the "uncorrupted"; the "virtuous" is mixed with the "vicious," the "unacceptable" is mixed with the "acceptable"; and the "good" is intertwined with the "bad." As Rev. Dr. Gardner Taylor once remarked, "If there's poison in a well of pure water, wherever one dips the dipper—if the water has poison in it—the dipper will come up with poisoned water." So, Paul says, "Do not conform."

This message is important for us today and it was especially important in the first century. At the time of this letter, Paul was in Corinth on his third missionary. He had never visited Rome but he was writing this church because in the first century, Christians were confused about their citizenship. A major question dealt with an allegiance to civil government. Loyalty was demanded by Claudius, who was the emperor of Rome, but loyalty was also demanded by the teachings of Jesus Christ. Jesus said, "Render unto Caesar the things which are Caesar's and to God the things which are God's" (Mark 12:17). What complicated this message for Christians is that they had a dual citizenship. They were citizens of time and also citizens of eternity. They lived on earth yet claimed "to be a colony in heaven." After all, Paul had affirmed: "For we know that if our earthly house of this tabernacle were dissolved, we have a building of God, an house not made with hands, eternal in the heavens." As such, Christians are what theologian Stanley Hauerwas calls "resident aliens." Although we live in an "earthly house," the physical body is not our eternal home. The Christian eschatological hope is "a day when we lay down our heavy burdens and sing and shout and tell the story, how we made it over." Christians in Rome were conscious of their dual citizenship—of being in the world but not of the world. They were like roads and highways in many American cities. For example, Highway 25 in Greenville (and Travelers Rest), South Carolina is the same as White Horse Road. In Boston, Massachusetts, Interstate 95 is the same as Route 128. In Richmond, Virginia, Route 1 is the same as Lombardy Street. In Birmingham, Alabama, Finley Avenue is also Highway 78 West. These are the same roads. They are both at the same time. So too, with these early Christians. They advocated what Martin Luther would later call a "doctrine of two kingdoms," namely the "kingdom of the world" and the "kingdom of Christ." As citizens in the "kingdom of the world," they had to pay taxes and obey the Roman law. As citizens in the "kingdom of Christ," they were required to obey a higher law—the law of love and righteousness. Paul gives these Christians encouragement because it was intimidating to live in a place like Rome. The Greeks and Romans overlooked them and made them feel insignificant and un-important.

Due to the military victories of Alexander the Great, the Roman Empire had become the most powerful nation in the Western world. It was once said, "All roads lead to Rome." There were big buildings, elaborate water baths, large temples, huge statues of gods and goddesses, and a long-standing tradition and culture of the Greeks that began over 700 years before Christianity.

Then, there were Christians—a helpless minority group who had neither prestige or power, trying to spread the *euangelion*, the "good news" about a religion appropriated from Jewish ideas of monotheism and mysticism. Christians refused to worship Greek and Roman gods because in ancient Judaism, the "Shema" recited twice daily says: "Hear, O Israel: the Lord our God, the Lord is one" (Deuteronomy 6:4).

Such ideas were incorporated at different times into Christianity and Paul reminds the Christians to be guided by their loyalties to the One who called them out of darkness to a marvelous Light. Also, he encourages them to be directed by the love of God and the aide of God's holy Spirit. Furthermore, be restrained by a conscience that is grounded in conviction and peace and then strengthened and empowered by habits of prayer and reflection.

Finally, Paul tells them to not surrender their supreme loyalty to any time-bound idea or earth-bound custom because at the heart of our universe, there is a higher reality to which we should conform. This higher reality is a greater Truth that is beyond our feeble rationality. We should conform to a greater Security that is beyond police protection and burglar alarm systems. We should conform to a greater Peace that is beyond the broken promises of peace treaties and United Nations agreements. We should conform to a greater Wealth that is richer and more satisfying than the hollow emptiness of our material accumulations. We should conform to a greater Love that is fuller and freer and fresher than the unpredictable fluctuation of human emotion. We should conform to a perfect Justice that transcends our arbitrary approximations of fairness. We should conform to a greater Help that is beyond all human options and all earthly hopes. "God is our help in ages past and hope for years to come, a Shelter from the stormy blast and our eternal home."[4]

By believing that God is able and by working to redeem and transform all that is wrong with our world, we can

---

4   Isaac Watts, "O God our Help in Ages Past," *The United Methodist Hymnal* (Nashville: The United Methodist Publishing House, 1989), 117.

work for the kingdom of God on earth as it is in heaven. "Do not conform to this world . . . Dare to be a new and a different person in all you think and do!" Amen.

Are You Willing to Pay the High Cost to Follow Jesus?

Dr. Echol L. Nix, Sr.

"Then said Jesus unto his disciples, If any man will come after me, let him deny himself, and take up his cross, and follow me." — St. Matthew 16:24

In the English language, there exist four different types of sentences as forms of expression. There is a declarative sentence. This type of sentence makes a statement and ends with a period. There is an exclamatory sentence. This type of sentence expresses excitement and ends with an exclamation mark. There is an imperative sentence. This type of sentence gives a command and ends with a period. Finally, there is the interrogative sentence. This type of sentence ends with a question mark. An interrogative sentence is the kind of sentence that is used as the sermon title: "Are you willing to pay the high cost to follow Jesus?"

The author of the book of Matthew was Matthew. He was also called Levi, a tax collector or publican. Matthew was a Jew who worked as a Roman government employee. Jews who collected taxes for Rome were despised as traitors to their own people. While sitting at the tax office, the receipt of custom, Matthew was called by Jesus to become one of His disciples. Matthew obeyed and gave up his business to follow Jesus. The question here is "Are you willing to pay the cost to follow Jesus?"

In the text, the writer Matthew alludes to three things that Jesus talked about in order to follow Him. They are: (1) Deny self, (2) Take up your cross, and (3) Follow Jesus. Most people fail to deny self because they don't fully understand self. The *American Heritage Dictionary* defines "self" as "the total essential or particular being of a person; the essential qualities distinguishing one person from another." [5] Self is a noun that is interchangeable with the pronouns "me," "myself," and "I." Self is that part which makes you think that you are right when you are wrong. It is also that part that will let you know that you are wrong or that you are right. Self often reminds me of a poem by Peter Winbrow:

The Man in the Glass

When you get what you want in your struggle for self,
And the world makes you king for a day,
Just go to a mirror and look at yourself,
And see what that man has to say.
For it isn't your father or mother or wife,

---

5 "Self." *American Heritage College Dictionary*. 3rd ed. 1997.

Whose judgment upon you must pass;

The fellow whose verdict counts most in your life,

Is the one staring back from the glass.

Some people might think that you're a straight-shootin'
chum,

And call you a wonderful guy,

But the man in the glass says you're only a bum,

If you can't look him straight in the eye.

He's the fellow to please never mind all the rest,

For he's with you clear up to the end.

And you've passed your most dangerous, difficult test,

If the guy in the glass is your friend.

You may fool the whole world down the pathway of
years,

And get pats on the back as you pass.

But your final reward will be heartaches and tears,

 If you've cheated the man in the glass.

Self can bring out the best in you as well as the worst in you. After having a definition of self, we should see better why Jesus said that self must be denied in order to follow Him. Denying self means to put self last in order to put Jesus first. Matthew 6:33 states, "But seek ye first the kingdom of God and his righteousness; and all these things shall be added unto you." To deny self requires a lesson in humility. Matthew 23:12 states, "And whosoever shall exalt himself shall be abased; and he that shall humble himself shall be exalted." To deny self will require one to take a self inventory.

Personally, I had many things to give up. What about you? Here is an inventory of some things:

A: Anger
B: Backsliding
C: Complaining
D: Dodging duties
E: Excessive alcohol
F: Fussing and fighting
G: Grudges
H: Hatred
I: Idolatry
J: Jealousy
K: Keeping up trouble
L: Lying
M: Mediocrity
N: Never saying "I'm sorry"
O: Oppressing others
P: Procrastinating
Q: Quick tongue
R: Resisting God
S: Stealing
T: Terrible temper
U: Using others
V: Violence
W: Wasting valuable time
X: Xeroxing others

Y: Yielding to temptation

Z: Zero understanding of God

There must be a complete change on the inside before one can surrender all. I am reminded of a Bible story where a rich young ruler came to Jesus with questions. The story goes:

> And when he [Jesus] was gone forth into the way, there came one running, and kneeled to him, and asked him, Good Master, what shall I do that I may inherit eternal life? And Jesus said unto him, Why callest thou me good? *there is* none good but one, *that is*, God. Thou knowest the commandments, Do not commit adultery, Do not kill, Do not steal, Do not bear false witness, Defraud not, Honor thy father and mother. And he answered and said unto him, Master, all these have I observed from my youth. Then Jesus beholding him loved him, and said unto him, One thing thou lackest: go thy way, sell whatsoever thou hast, and give to the poor, and thou shalt have treasure in heaven: and come take up the cross, and follow me. And he [the young ruler] was sad at that saying, and went away grieved: for he had great possessions (Mark 10:17–22).

The rich man found it hard to "surrender all."

After self is denied, we must take up the cross and follow Jesus. Jesus stated in Matthew 10:38, "And he that taketh not his cross, and followeth after me is not worthy of me." In Matthew 10:39 Jesus also stated, "He that findeth his life shall lose it; and he that loseth his life for my sake shall find it." It has often been stated, "No cross, no crown." Crucifixion on the cross was practiced by Greek-speaking Christians (in the East) and by Latin-speaking Christians (in the West). In the Roman Era, there were four crosses of significance.

First of all, there was the Latin Cross (or *crux ordinaria*), a symbol of Christianity even though it was used as a pagan symbol for millennia before the Christian church was founded. Second, there was St. Anthony's cross also called the "Cross of Tau," and named after the Greek letter it resembles. It is thought to have originated with ancient Egyptians. Third, there was St. Andrew's, (or in Latin *crux decussata*) which was a symbol in the form of a diagonal cross (X). Saint Andrew is said to have been martyred on such a cross. Finally, the Greek Cross, also known as the *crux immissa*, was used especially by Eastern Orthodox churches after the middle ages. The hymn writer asks: "Must Jesus bear the Cross alone and all the world go free? There is a cross for everyone and there is a cross for me." The Word of God further states: "Greater love hath no man than this, that a man lay down his life for his friends" (St. John 15:13).

For Jesus, the cross was symbolic of love. The sins of the world were attached to Jesus' cross. This is why John the Baptist could say, "Behold the Lamb of God, which taketh away the sin of the world" (St. John 1:29). All types of sin were attached to Jesus' cross. Attached was the sin of omission and the sin of commission. Sin can be classified in three categories. They are: (1) the lust of the flesh, (2) the lust of the eyes, (3) the pride of life (I John 2:16). I can see why the song writer could say, "What a friend we have in Jesus, all our sins and griefs to bear! What a privilege to carry, everything to God in prayer! O what peace we often forfeit, O what needless pain we bear, all because we do not carry, everything to God in prayer!"

Jesus had the weight of the world on His shoulders. Therefore, our crosses are much lighter than Jesus' cross. Your cross could be sadness and constant weeping, but the words of the psalmist offer hope: "Weeping may endure for a night, but joy cometh in the morning" (Psalm 30:5). Are you lied on or talked about? Never forget the words of Jesus, "Blessed are ye, when *men* shall revile you, and persecute *you*, and shall say all manner of evil against you falsely, for my sake. Rejoice, and be exceeding glad: for great *is* your reward in heaven: for so persecuted they the prophets which were before you" (Matthew 5:11–12).

Are you carrying a heavy load? Remember the words of Jesus, "Come unto me, all *ye* that labour and are heavy laden, and I will give you rest. Take my yoke upon you, and learn of me; for I am meek and lowly in heart: and ye shall find rest unto your souls. For my yoke *is* easy, and my burden is light" (Matthew 11:28–30). Are you impatient? If so, read Isaiah 40:31, "But they that wait upon the Lord shall renew their strength; they shall mount up with wings as eagles; they shall run and not be weary, and they shall walk, and not faint." Are you in trouble and need relief? Remember St. John 14:1: "Let not your heart be troubled: ye believe in God, believe also in me." Are you physically or spiritually weak and need more strength for the journey ahead? Remember the words of Paul in Philippians 4:13. "I can do all things through Christ who strengthens me."

Are you in distress and need comfort? David said in Psalm 23, "The Lord is my shepherd; I shall not want. He maketh me to lie down in green pastures: he leadeth me beside the still waters. He restoreth my soul: he leadeth me in the paths of righteousness for his name's sake. Yea, though I walk through the valley of the shadow of death, I will fear no evil: for thou art with me; thy rod and thy staff they comfort me. Thou preparest a table before me in the presence of mine enemies: thou anointest my head with oil; my cup runneth over. Surely goodness and mercy shall follow me all the days of my life: and I will dwell in the house of the Lord forever."

Sadness or depression could be weighing you down. Again, remember the words of David: "Make a joyful noise unto the Lord, all ye lands. Serve the Lord with gladness: come before his presence with singing. Know ye that the Lord he is God: it is he that hath made us, and not we ourselves; we are his people, and the sheep of his pasture. Enter into his gates with thanksgiving, and into his courts with praise: be thankful unto him, and bless his name. For the Lord is good; his mercy is everlasting; and his truth endureth to all generations" (Psalm 100). If your cross is sickness, read Isaiah 53:4–5: "Surely he hath borne our griefs, and carried our sorrows, yet we did esteem him stricken, smitten of God and afflicted. But he was wounded for our transgressions, he was bruised for our iniquities: the chastisement of our peace was upon him; and with his stripes we are healed."

If your cross is someone's death or someone who's dying, contemplate the words of Paul in II Corinthians 5:1: "For we know that if our earthly house of this tabernacle were dissolved, we have a building of God, an house not made with hands, eternal in the heavens." In order to bear your cross, you might need a little more faith. According to the writer of Hebrew: "Now faith is the substance of things hoped for, the evidence of things not seen" (Hebrew 11:1). It is possible that some type of sin could be a cross, weighing you down. David also stated in Psalm 51:1–11:

> Have mercy upon me, O God, according to thy lovingkindness: according to the multitude of thy tender mercies blot out my transgressions. Wash me thoroughly from mine iniquity, and cleanse me from my sin. For I acknowledge my transgressions: and my sin is ever before me. Against thee, thee only, have I sinned, and done this evil in thy sight: that thou mightest be justified when thou

speakest, and be clear when thou judgest. Behold I was shapen in iniquity, and in sin did my mother conceive me. Behold, thou desirest truth in the inward parts: and in the hidden part thou shalt make me to know wisdom. Purge me with hyssop, and I shall be clean: wash me, and I shall be whiter than snow. Make me to hear joy and gladness; that the bones which thou hast broken may rejoice. Hide thy face from my sins, and blot out all mine iniquities. Create in me a clean heart, O God; and renew a right spirit within me. Cast me not away from thy presence; and take not thy holy spirit from me.

Do you have a problem with trusting? I urge you to trust in God and read Proverbs 3:5–6: "Trust in the Lord with all thine heart; and lean not unto thine own understanding. In all thy ways acknowledge him, and he shall direct thy paths." Some crosses may be "multiple problems" which seem unbearable at times. You may feel as though God has forgotten you or feel like your prayers are not being answered. If this is a cross, read Psalm 37:4: "Delight thyself also in the Lord; and he shall give thee the desires of thine heart." If fear is a cross— fear of going outdoors, fear of crowds, fear of loneliness, or simply fear of the unknown—reflect on Psalm 27:1. It states: "The Lord is my light and my salvation; whom shall I fear? The Lord is the strength of my life; of whom shall I be afraid?"

Someone's cross may be demons. If so, rest assured!

James 4:7 reminds us: "Submit yourselves therefore to God. Resist the devil, and he will flee from you." Do you have difficulty praising or thanking God? Psalm 34:1–4 may help: "I will bless the Lord at all times: his praise shall continually be in my mouth. My soul shall make her boast in the Lord: the humble shall hear thereof, and be glad. O magnify the Lord with me, and let us exalt his name together. I sought the Lord, and he heard me, and delivered me from all my fears."

Are you a doubter? If so, read Matthew 7:7, "Ask, and it shall be given you; seek and ye shall find; knock, and it shall be opened unto you." Are you confused about where to go for help during times of need? Have you turned to a friend or loved one and did not find the help you needed? Remember Psalm 121:1–2: "I will lift up mine eyes unto the hills, from whence cometh my help; my help cometh from the Lord, which made heaven and earth." Do you feel alone, despite having family, friends, classmates or co-workers? If loneliness is weighing you down, know that God cares for you and that He will be with you: "Fear not; for I am with thee: be not dismayed; for I am thy God: I will strengthen thee; yea, I will help thee; yea, I will uphold thee with the right hand of my righteousness" (Isaiah 41:10).

The last point is to "follow Jesus." There have been many men, women, boys, and girls throughout history who have served as models yet followers of others. Presidents have followed other presidents. Kings have followed other kings. Many athletes have followed other athletes. Many movie stars have tried to follow other movie stars. Many politicians and pastors have followed their predecessors. Outstanding teachers have followed other outstanding teachers. Outstanding soldiers have followed other outstanding soldiers. Joshua followed behind Moses as a great leader. Elisha followed behind Elijah as a great prophet. Eleazar followed behind Aaron as a priest. However, the question is "Are you willing to pay the high cost to follow Jesus?"

If you are committed to following Jesus, you will experience trials and tribulations. You may be talked about, lied on, abused, or misused. You may experience lonely days and nights, but Jesus said, "Follow me." Your enemies may smile in your face and talk about you behind your back, but Jesus said, "Follow me." He also said in Matthew 5:44: "Love your enemies, bless them that curse you, do good to them that hate you, and pray for them which despitefully use you, and persecute you."

One who follows Jesus must be willing to forgive and forget. According to Matthew 18:21–22: "Then came Peter to him, and said, Lord, how oft shall my brother sin against me, and I forgive him? till seven times? Jesus saith unto him, I say not unto thee, Until seven times: but, Until seventy times seven." One who follows Jesus should have a shining light. Jesus told His disciples, "Ye are the light of the world. A city that is set on a hill cannot be hid. Neither do men light a candle, and put it under a bushel, but on a candlestick; and it giveth light unto all that are in the house. Let your light so shine before men, that they may see your good works, and glorify your Father which is in heaven" (Matthew 5:14–16). For one to follow Jesus, he or she must be truthful. Jesus said, "I am the way, the truth, and the life: no man cometh unto the Father, but by me" (St. John 14:6). For one to follow Jesus, he or she should have a pure heart. Jesus said, "Blessed are the pure in heart: for they shall see God" (Matthew 5:8). One who follows Jesus should be meek and not weak. Jesus said, "Blessed are the meek: for they shall inherit the earth" (Matthew 5:5). One who follows Jesus should have a zeal for righteousness. Jesus said, "Blessed are they which do hunger and thirst after righteousness: for they shall be filled" (Matthew 5:6).

Finally, one who follows Jesus should have love in his or her heart. Jesus said in Mark 12:30–31: "And thou shalt love the Lord thy God with all thy heart, and with all thy soul, and with all thy mind, and with all thy strength: this is the first commandment. And the second is like, namely this, Thou shalt love thy neighbour as thyself. There is no other commandment greater than these."

There are many who gave their lives in order to follow Jesus. For example, John the Baptist, a forerunner of Jesus, was beheaded for the cause of following Him. Stephen, one of the first deacons in the early church, was stoned to death for the same cause. John Mark was decapitated or torn to pieces by the people of Alexandria because he was a follower of Jesus. After Matthias was chosen to fill the vacancy left by Judas, Matthias was stoned at Jerusalem and then beheaded for the cause of following Jesus. Luke, the only Gentile writer in the New Testament to author two books, namely Luke and Acts, was hanged on an olive tree in Greece for the cause of following Jesus. Peter was condemned to death in Rome and crucified upside down for following Jesus. The Apostle Paul, also called Saul, went to the Roman Emperor Nero's chopping block, losing his head for following Jesus. There are many more men (and women) who were martyred. I have given only a brief list of the many Christians who gave their lives for the sake of following Jesus. Are you willing to pay the high cost to follow Jesus? Let me testify:

> I have decided to follow Jesus;
> I have decided to follow Jesus;
> I have decided to follow Jesus;
> No turning back, no turning back.

> Though I may wonder, I still will follow;
> Though I may wonder, I still will follow;
> Though I may wonder, I still will follow;
> No turning back, no turning back.

> The world behind me, the cross before me;
> The world behind me, the cross before me;
> The world behind me, the cross before me;

No turning back, no turning back.

Though none go with me, still I will follow;
Though none go with me, still I will follow;
Though none go with me, still I will follow;
No turning back, no turning back.

Will you decide now to follow Jesus?
Will you decide now to follow Jesus?
Will you decide now to follow Jesus;
No turning back, no turning back.

Diamonds in the Rough

Dr. Echol L. Nix, Sr.

"But we have this treasure in earthen vessels, that the excellency of the power may be of God, and not of us." — II Corinthians 4:7

Diamonds have been prized throughout history for their unusual beauty, sharpness, and hardness. However, diamonds are rough and uneven when discovered in nature. They do not show all of their beauty as rough stones. They must go through a process of being cut, shaped, and polished into a beautiful form and fashion. The purpose of this sermon is to show the similarity of a diamond with that of a Christian. In order to achieve my purpose, I would like to discuss three points: (1) the process of forming a diamond compared with the process of Christian formation, (2) the hardness and sharpness of a diamond compared with the hardness and sharpness of a Christian, and (3) the beauty of a diamond compared with the beauty of a Christian.

The first point I will discuss is the process of forming a

diamond compared with the formation of a true Christian. Diamonds are formed deep down in the mantle of the earth's surface by carbon being crystallized from tremendous heat and pressure. One way these stones can reach the earth's surface is by way of volcanic eruptions. Even in nature God has a way of letting that which is considered the worse become the best. God has a way of taking those who are lost, unlucky, left out and considered the "least of these" and lets them rise from the bottom to the top. The *World Book Encyclopedia* states that the first diamonds were found in the sand and gravel of stream beds. These are called alluvial diamonds. Later, diamonds were found deep in the earth, in rock formations called pipes, thought to be the throats of extinct volcanoes. The rock in which diamonds are found is called blue ground. But even in South African mines, the world's richest source for gems, including diamonds, many tons of blue ground must be taken from deep in the earth, crushed and sorted to obtain one small diamond. There is a special saw used to cut a diamond. Diamond cutting begins when a skilled crafts-worker saws a rough diamond in half. He or she uses a thin circular saw that holds diamond dust. The corners are then rounded by rubbing together a spinning diamond and a stationary one. As jewelers learned more about diamonds they discovered shapes that produced the greatest brilliance. A popular cut often seen today is the round shape with fifty-eight facets which is called the "brilliant cut." Cutting and polishing the rough diamond is a slow process. It must be executed by highly skilled workers. Once finished, a diamond is then ready for display or purchase.

Nevertheless, Christians also go through a similar process as diamonds. We do not start out as a finished product. We all start out like rough diamonds. Romans 3:23 states: "For all have sinned, and come short of the glory of God." First, I speak of myself. I was like John Newton's description of a "wretch" and in need of God's amazing grace." Yes, it is amazing how God can take sinners and make saints. It is mind-boggling how God can find treasure in earthen vessels.

The sixteenth century Protestant reformer Martin Luther wondered how unrighteous humanity can be made righteous. The answer for him was Romans 1:12: "For therein is the righteousness of God revealed from faith to faith: as it is written, the just shall live by faith." For Paul and for Luther, justification of a sinner is through faith. One step in the process of justification and in God's plan of salvation is confession. Romans 10:9–10 states, "That if thou shalt confess with thy mouth the Lord Jesus, and shalt believe in thine heart that God hath raised him from the dead, thou shalt be saved. For with the heart man believeth unto righteousness; and with the mouth confession is made unto salvation." Confessing is acknowledging that I am a sinner and need Jesus as my personal Savior.

Another step in the process of Christian formation is

conversion. Conversion relates to faith and repentance. Faith is believing that you can do something when others say that you cannot. Repentance means to be sorry for your sins. It means to come to oneself before you can start living for God and serving others. Acts 3:19–20 states: "Repent ye therefore, and be converted, that your sins may be blotted out, when the times of refreshing shall come from the presence of the Lord; And he shall send Jesus Christ, which before was preached unto you."

Next is regeneration. Regeneration refers to a "new birth" or being "born again." In St. John 3:3 Jesus said to Nicodemus: "Verily, verily, I say unto thee, Except a man be born again, he cannot see the kingdom of God." There must be a change from the "old" to the "new." The old you must die in order for the new to live. Paul states in II Corinthians 5:17: "Therefore if any man be in Christ, he is a new creature: old things are passed away; behold, all things are become new." A song says: "Have thine own way Lord, have thine own way. Thou art the potter, I am the clay. Mold me and make me after thy will, while I am waiting, yielded and still." A convert may be able to exclaim: "I looked at my hands and my hands looked new, I looked at my feet and they did too." The new birth can mean a loss of interest in the things you used to do and the places you used to go.

Another important step is adoption. Adoption refers to membership in God's family. In Ephesians 1:5, Paul states: "Having predestinated us unto the adoption of children by Jesus Christ to himself, according to the good pleasure of his will." The final step in the process of Christian formation is sanctification. John Wesley, the nineteenth century theologian and founder of the Methodist Church distinguished between salvation and sanctification. After one is saved, Wesley thought one should "go on to perfection." "Going on to perfection" is what he means by sanctification. Wesley's doctrine of sanctification is connected to salvation. II Thessalonians 2:13 states: "But we are bound to give thanks always to God for you, brethren beloved of the Lord, because God hath from the beginning chosen you to salvation through sanctification of the Spirit and belief of the truth." As faithful followers, we must be willing to do all we can and what we can. The songwriter says: "You ought to live so God can use you anywhere, anytime."

Second, the hardness and sharpness of a diamond can be compared with the hardness and sharpness of a Christian. According to excavations and other evidence, a diamond is one of the hardest and most enduring stones in the world. In like manner, a Christian must also demonstrate hardness like a diamond. A Christian must be able to withstand heartaches, pain, trials and tribulations. Also, Christians are often ostracized, criticized, scandalized and scrutinized. It's not easy being a Christian. Jesus said in Matthew 5:44: "Love your enemies, bless them that curse you, do good to them that hate you, and pray for them which despitefully use you and persecute you."

Paul discusses the difficulties of a Christian in terms of the hardness of a good soldier: "Endure hardness as a good soldier of Jesus Christ." In addition to maintaining hardness, we must maintain sharpness. It has been stated that a diamond is so sharp that it can cut glass or another diamond. According to the Bible, the word of God is sharp and "it cuts like a two-edged sword." A friend and a very smart, former student of mine, Elder Larry Lewis rightly remarked: "The word of God needs to be in our heads and our hearts." Paul stated in Philippians 2:5 "Let this mind be in you, which was also in Christ Jesus."

As a Christian, we must study the Word of God. Unfortunately, too many Bibles get dusty and too many minds get rusty. The New Testament scholar D. A. Carson once wrote:

> The Bible reveals the mind of God, the state of man, the way of salvation, the happiness of believers. Its doctrines are holy, its precepts are binding, its histories are true, and its decisions are immutable. Read it to be wise, believe it to be save and practice it to be holy. It contains light to direct, food to support you, and comfort to cheer you. It is the traveler's map, the pilgrim's staff, the pilot's compass, the soldier's sword, and the Christian's charter. Here paradise is restored, Heaven opened, and the gates of hell disclosed. Christ is its grand subject, our good its design and the glory of God its end. It should fill the memory, rule the heart and guide the feet. Read it

slowly, frequently, prayerfully, sincerely, and spiritually. It is a mind of wealth, a paradise of glory, and a river of pleasure. It involves the highest responsibility, will reward the greatest labor, and condemn all who trifle with its sacred contents.

The last point is the beauty of a diamond compared to a Christian lifestyle. A diamond sparkles and shines. Likewise, a Christian should also glow and shine like a diamond. In Matthew 5:16 Jesus said: "Let your light so shine before men, that they may see your good works, and glorify your Father which is in heaven." A Christian's life should shine like a diamond in a world of darkness, chaos and trouble. Many parents have given up on their children because of the many challenges facing this generation. Teenagers also have children, which produces its own set of challenges. Sociologists note that every society has social problems that require attention from political, social and religious leaders. Further, thousands of students drop out of high school and get involved in too many unwholesome activities. There is so much darkness and hopelessness. Many streets and schools are like war zones and violence is rampant in many places. Many so-called Christians have lost their glow and are hiding in the crowd. We have too many counterfeit Christians just like counterfeit diamonds. We have too many marking time and not making time. I agree with Dr. Benjamin Mays who said: "I would rather die and go to hell by choice than to stumble into heaven by following the crowd." The wrong crowd can get you into more trouble than you will be able to get out of.

Finally, in spite of your shortcomings, I encourage you to shine and to sparkle. Abraham was flawed by saying Sarah was his sister and not his wife. However, God made a covenant with him and Abraham is considered the "father of the faithful." Jacob stole his brother Esau's birthright but he became the father of the twelve tribes of Israel. Moses murdered an Egyptian and buried him in the sand, but he still became a great lawgiver and deliverer. David, who was considered a "man after God's own heart" arranged for Uriah the Hittite to be killed in battle, after sleeping with Uriah's wife Bathsheba. Yet, David was considered one of the greatest kings of Israel and publicly confessed his mistake in Psalm 51. In all these cases and many more (involving both men and women), God saw diamonds in the rough.

It is quite possible that you, too, are a diamond in the rough. It could be that you need a little (or a lot) more molding, shaping and making. A songwriter wrote: "Please be patient with me, God is not through with me yet." On April 1, 1984 the Master looked beyond my faults and saw my needs. The Rev. Johnny Carter, a long time friend of mine, would say that, "God looked through dirty water and spotted dry land." He saw a rough, uncut and unfit diamond that needed a lot of molding, shaping and making. I thank God for not giving up on me when others said that I would not succeed. I thank God for being a friend that I could always depend on. If I could speak 10,000 languages, I would thank God in each language. In Aramaic, I would say "*Todi/Dodi*. In Japanese, I would say *Arigato*; if I could thank Him in German, it would be *Danke schön*; in Spanish, it would be *Gracias*; in Russian, *Spasibo*; if I could thank Him in Portuguese, it would be *Obrigado*; in Danish, it would be *Mange tak*; if I could thank Him in Italian, it would be *Grazie*; if I could thank him in French, it would be *Merci beaucoup*; in Hebrew, *Toda raba*; and if I could thank Him in Greek, it would be *Efcharisto*! In my native English, I cannot thank Him enough . . . all day . . . and all night, Thank you, Lord! You've been so good! You brought me out! You made a way!

If you want to know more about this Way Maker, I'll gladly share my knowledge and personal experiences. There have been many men and women listed as great in history, such as Socrates, Plato, Aristotle, Ruth, Deborah, and many others. However, none could match the greatness of Jesus. He can be crowned as a King, Priest, Prophet, God, Man, Spirit, and Christ.

We can *Crown Him King*: The kings in Israel's United Kingdom were Saul, David, and Solomon. Kings in the Northern Kingdom were Jeroboam I, Nadab, Baasha, Elah, Zimri, Omri, Ahab, Ahaziah, Joram, Jehu, Jehoahaz, Jehoash, Jeroboam II, Zechariah, Shallum, Menahem, Pehahiah, Pekah, Hoshea. The Kings in the Southern Kingdom were Rehoboam, Abijah, Asa, Jehoshaphat, Jehoram,

Ahaziah, Athaliah, Joash, Amaziah, Uzziah, Jotham, Ahaz, Hezekiah, Manasseh, Amon, Josiah, Jehoahaz, Jehoiakim, Jehoiachin, and Zedekiah. However, none could be called the "King of Kings" and "Lord of Lords."

We can *Crown Him Priest*: There were many priests, such as Aaron, Eleazar, Phinehas, Eli, Samuel, and others but none could follow the order of Melchizedek but Jesus, Priest of the most high God.

We can *Crown Him Prophet*: There were prophets listed in the Bible such as Isaiah, Jeremiah, Ezekiel, Daniel, Hosea, Joel, Amos, Obediah, Jonah, Micah, Nahum, Habakkuk, Zephaniah, Haggai, Zechariah, and Malachi. There were non-writing prophets such as Ahijah, Elijah, Elisha, Micaiah, Nathan, and Gad but Jesus would be considered a "Prophet like Moses."

We can *Crown Him God and Man*: As divine He was begotten by God but as a man, He was conceived by Mary. As a man He got lonely but as God He was never alone. One songwriter said, "No, never alone. No, never alone. He promised never to leave me, never to leave me alone." He never went to medical school but he healed many with infirmities and all manner of sickness. He was not rich according to most standards. Luke 9:58 says: "Foxes have holes, birds of the air have nests but the Son of Man has nowhere to lay his head." He was not a bartender but He turned water into wine. He was not a navigator but He stood up to the wind and said "Peace be still." He was not a chef but He took two fish and five loaves of bread and fed multitudes and had food left over. He spoke to men who were able to see and they became blind. He spoke to blind men and they received their sight. He spoke to a fig tree and it died. He spoke to a woman bent over and she straightened up.

We can *Crown Him Spirit*: They that worship Him should worship Him in Spirit and in Truth. His Spirit is higher than up, lower than down, quicker than at once, and faster than now. His Spirit elevates, activates, motivates, stimulates, cultivates, consolates and rejuvenates. Finally, we can *Crown Him Christ*, the Anointed One.

From a Christian theological perspective, Jesus is a part of salvation history in each book of the bible:

In Genesis 3:15, the Seed of the woman.

In Exodus 12:3, the Passover Lamb.

In Leviticus 17:11, the Atoning Sacrifice.

In Numbers 20:8, 11, the Smitten Rock.

In Deuteronomy 18:15, a Prophet like Moses.

In Joshua 5:15, the Captain of the Lord's Host.

In Judges 2:18, the Divine Deliverer.

In Ruth 3:12, the Kinsman Redeemer.

In 1 Samuel 2:10, the Anticipated Anointed One.

In 2 Samuel 7:14, the Son of David.

In 1 Kings 8:23, the God of heaven and the God of earth.

In 2 Kings 42:42–44, the Bread that fed the multitude.

In 1 Chronicles 28:20, the Builder of the Temple.

In 2 Chronicles 30:1, the Passover that Hezekiah talked about concerning Israel.

In Ezra 6:14, 15, the Restorer of the Temple.

In Nehemiah 6:15, the Restorer of the Nation.

In Esther 4:14, the Preserver of the Nation.

In Job 19:25, the Risen and Returning Redeemer.

In Psalms 150:6, the Praise of Israel.

In Proverbs 8:22–23, our Wisdom demonstrated.

In Ecclesiastes 12:11, the Great Teacher.

In the Song of Solomon 5:10, the Fairest of Ten Thousand.

In Isaiah 53:11, the Suffering Servant.

In Jeremiah 23:6, the Lord of our Righteousness.

In Lamentations 3:28–30, the Man of Sorrows.

In Ezekiel 1:26, the Throne Sitter.

In Daniel 9:25, the Coming Messiah.

In Hosea 3:1, the Lover of the Unfaithful.

In Joel 3:16, the Hope of Israel.

In Amos 9:13, the Husbandman.

In Obadiah 1:17, the Judge upon Mount Zion.

In Jonah 2:10, the Resurrected One.

In Micah 5:2, the Ruler in Israel.

In Nahum 2:1, the Avenger.

In Habakkuk 1:13, the Holy God.

In Zephaniah 3:15, the King of Israel.

In Haggai 2:7, the Desire of Nations.

In Zechariah 3:8, the Righteous Branch.

In Malachi 4:2, the Sun of Righteousness.

In Matthew 2:2, the King of the Jews.

In Mark 10:45, the Servant of the Lord.

In Luke 19:10, the Son of Man.

In John 1:1, the Son of God.

In Acts 1:10, the Ascended Lord.

In Romans 1:17, the believer's Righteousness.

In 1 Corinthians 1:30, the One who sanctifies.

In 2 Corinthians 12:9, Sufficient Help.

In Galatians 2:4, the Giver of liberty.

In Ephesians 1:22, the Exalted Head of the church.

In Philippians 1:26, the Christian's Joy.

In Colossians 2:9, the Fullness of the living God.

In 1 Thessalonians 4:15, 16, our Returning Lord.

In 2 Thessalonians 1:7–9, the World's Returning Judge.

In 1 Timothy 4:10, the Christian's Preserver.

In 2 Timothy 4:8, the Rewarder of Crowns.

In Titus 2:13, the Blessed Hope.

In Philemon 17, the Substitute.

In Hebrews 4:15, the High Priest.

In James 1:5, the Giver of Wisdom.

In 1 Peter 2:6, the solid Rock.

In 2 Peter 1:4, the Precious Promise.

In 1 John 1:1, the Word of Life.

In 2 John 1:2–3 the Truth.

In 3 John 1:3–4, the Personification of Truth.

In Jude 1:24–25, the Believer's Security.

In Revelation 19:11–16, the King of Kings and Lord of Lords.

There is No Place Like Home

Dr. Echol L. Nix, Sr.

"And when he had spent all, there arose a mighty famine in that land; and he began to be in want. And he arose, and came to his father. But when he was yet a great way off, his father saw him, and had compassion, and ran, and fell on his neck, and kissed him."
— Luke 15:14, 20

Dr. Luke is identified as the author of the above text. He was the beloved physician alluded to in Colossians 4:14. Luke wrote his gospel with a twofold purpose—a historical purpose and a spiritual purpose. Luke was the only Gentile writer to author two books in the Bible, both in the New Testament. These books are St. Luke and Acts. The book of Luke is the forty-second book of the Bible and consists of twenty-four chapters, 1,151 verses, and 25,944 words. There are many parables, social and ethical themes and different illustrations used to communicate spiritual truth or morals told throughout the book. However, the parable that I will focus on is a familiar one to many people. It is called "The Parable of the Prodigal Son."

The word "prodigal" means "wastefully extravagant." This concept is not limited to a particular gender, race, nationality or social class. Anyone could very well be a prodigal. This may be your story or it may be my story. To illustrate, I would like to use three points: (1) I had it. (2) I lost it. (3) Now, I want it back. Let us look at the first point: "I Had It." In the text, Jesus is talking and his parable refers to a man who had two sons. The number two indicates that there is a difference. The younger son said to his father, "Give me the portion of goods that falleth to me." So the father divided his living to his oldest and youngest sons. While reading this story, one cannot be certain whether or not the young man had a good relationship with his father. It is mighty good when children can have a good relationship with their parents because I have seen unfortunate situations when many do not. I have read about fathers and sons killing one another and I have seen mothers and daughters fighting and disrespecting each other. However, it seems as though this young man had a nice home with love, comfort, fellowship and money. I would say that he had it "made in the shade." Experience has taught me that it is not good for one to get everything so easy. A colloquial phrase is: "You can't appreciate the sunshine until you have experienced some rain." Too many people want something for nothing and many want too much too fast. According to the text, the younger son received his entire portion from his father and took his journey into a far country where he wasted his substance with "riotous living" (verse 13). When I was growing up in Montevallo, Alabama, I thought the grass was greener on the other side. I could not wait to leave home. I could not wait to graduate from high school and receive a football scholarship to Mississippi Valley State University in Itta Bena, Mississippi. Being a poor country boy who had not traveled much, I thought that three hundred miles from home was a far country. I anticipated it was just as far as Spain, Canada, France, Japan or any other country. However, throughout the years, I have realized that a far country could be your home or my home. When there is no love, respect, or discipline in a home it could very well be a far country. A far country could also be found in church where one is not being spiritually fed or nourished or where there is confusion and disturbance in the congregation. A far country could be a school where no learning is taking place. A far country could be a community that has lost its sense of unity or spirit.

The second point is: "I Lost It." According to the King James Version, the young man spent all he had with "riotous living." The New Revised Standard Version says "he squandered his property in dissolute living." Suddenly, there arose a mighty famine in the land and he began to be in want. If you want to see your real friends, call them when you are desperate and needy. You might experience what the prodigal son experienced. He found out that when he had money, he had friends. Throughout the years, I have discovered the same. The prodigal son left his father's house and ended up in a pigpen. The young man wanted to venture out but the far country was further than he anticipated, estimated, and calculated. It seems as though when his money left, his friends left. My philosophy is to never trust a so-called friend any farther than you can see with your eyes closed tightly.

At this point in the story the young man is down and out with the blues. Not only is he in a very bad shape financially, but the country is also in a recession and perhaps in a depression due to a severe famine. As a result, the boy does something that no Jew would have thought of doing. Swine is considered unclean and a Jewish person has nothing to do with swine as stated in the Mosaic law. The young man had to stoop to a level of living with hogs—which was humiliating for any Jew. I have found that it is never good to say what you won't do in life because what "I won't do" may turn into what "I will do" and what "I have to do." I have seen innocent girls and boys unexpectedly turn to a life in drugs, crime and prostitution. It hurts me as I write this sermon because so many young people as well as old people fall into the same path and experience similar problems as the prodigal son. It is troubling because many never make an effort to raise their level of consciousness which could help them recover and return.

The third point is: "I Want It Back." The theological term that means "knowledge gained after experience" is "*a posteriori.*" The prodigal son had this kind of knowledge. After being on his own for a while, he decided to return home. The text says, "He came to himself." He said, "How many hired servants of my father's have bread enough and to spare, and I perish with hunger! I will arise and go to my father, and will say unto him, Father, I have sinned against heaven, and before thee, And am no more worthy to be called thy son: make me as one of thy hired servants" (Luke15:17–19). The prodigal son would agree wholeheartedly with Dorothy from the twentieth century American film *Wizard of Oz*. After Dorothy clicked her heels three times, she also repeated three times: "There is no place like home." I am truly glad that the young man came to himself.

Some people live their entire life and never come to themselves. Many are trapped in the stronghold of unwholesome activities and never make a change. Sometimes a pigpen can get their attention but it's better to find oneself before that happens. This prodigal son was big enough to admit to his mistakes and smart enough to learn from them. Most of all, he was willing to correct his mistakes and move on with his life. According to the Bible, "He arose, and went to his father. But when he was yet a great way off, his father saw him, and had compassion, and ran, and fell on his neck, and kissed him" (15:20). I imagine this was a moment of excitement and gladness for the prodigal son and his father. This parable is rightly called a "parable of great joy," along with the parable of the lost coin and the lost sheep, also in Luke 15. In spite of the prodigal son's crippling circumstances, he was determined to go home. It thrills me to see more and more families across our nation and around the world come together. Personally, I'm happy that my family members from the Nix and Tolbert families have made a covenant that every two years there will be a family reunion—a time to return to the old landmark to meet one another, greet one another, reminisce with one another, love one another, and worship with one another. Family reunions can be meaningful and joyous occasions.

Nevertheless, I am so glad that the prodigal son's earthly father was compassionate like our Heavenly Father is with us. God is the One who looks beyond our faults to see our needs. As a loving and compassionate Father, God is ready to receive with welcome arms that prodigal son, prodigal daughter, prodigal husband, prodigal wife, and all others who have sinned and come short of the glory of God! "If we confess our sins, he is faithful and just to forgive us our sins, and to cleanse us from all unrighteousness" (I John 1:9). The unknown author of "God's Minute" helps us understand the importance of how we spend our time:

> I have only just a minute.
> Sixty seconds are in it.

Forced upon me.

And I can't refuse it.

I didn't seek it and I didn't choose it,

But it's up to me to use it.

I must suffer if I lose it,

Give account if I abuse it.

Just a tiny, little minute,

But eternity is in it.

Life as Worship Service

DR. ECHOL L. NIX, JR.

"And he called to him his twelve disciples and gave them authority over unclean spirits, to cast them out and to heal every disease and every infirmity."
— St. Matthew 10:1

The Christian life is multi-faceted and there is disagreement over Christian identity. What are the characteristics of a Christian? How should a Christian act? What should a Christian do? What shouldn't a Christian do? For many, the answers become a list of "Do's" and "Don'ts." For others, the answers are shaped by the popular question, "What would Jesus do?" But it's difficult to know exactly what Jesus would do. Christianity is a complex, cultural and historical religion, just as other religions. The study of religion helps us to explore the beliefs, practices, and symbols of religious traditions and to further explore questions about the meaning of life and death. Christianity, as with other religions, seeks to provide answers to normative questions.

One normative question is, "Why is there something and not nothing?" This was the question of the Greek philosopher Parmenides and is one that we still wrestle with today. God created the world, but why? And then, we are created in the image of God (or the *imago Dei*, in Latin), but why are we here? What is the purpose of life? What is our *raison d'être* (reason for being)? There are many sources, sacred books, wisdom literature, theories and so forth to help us clarify these issues and the Bible is one of these sources. We find, in both the Old and New Testaments, a relationship between worship and work— which are two activities central to a Christian lifestyle.

In Deuteronomy, the commandment to love God is issued by Moses: "Hear O Israel, the Lord our God is one, and you shall love the Lord your God with all your heart and with all your soul and with all your might" (4:1). In Matthew 22:36, Jesus reiterates this commandment and adds a corollary to it. "And one of them, a lawyer asked him a question to test him. 'Teacher, which commandment in the law is the greatest?' He said to him, 'You shall love the Lord your God with all your heart, and with all your soul and with all your mind.' This is the greatest and first commandment. And a second is like it. 'You shall love your neighbor as yourself.'" Jesus' life and ministry are perfect examples of both word and deed. He glorified God, and simultaneously served his neighbor. His vertical relationship with God was matched with a horizontal relationship with humanity. In reference to this relationship,

John, the beloved disciple, writes about love in both the Gospel of John and in the Book of I John. In I John 4:20, he states: "For those who do not love a brother or sister, whom they have seen, cannot love God when they have not seen." It follows that those who love God must love their brothers and sisters, also.

In the Gospel according to John, John presents Jesus first of all, as the embodiment of God's Word. John 1:14 says: "The Word became flesh." Second, John presents Jesus as a demonstration of God's love. John 3:16 says: "For God so loved the world that He gave His only Son." After Jesus appeared on the historical scene, he called disciples to assist him in His work. This call is found in Matthew 4: "As he walked by the Sea of Galilee, he saw two brothers, Simon, who is called Peter and Andrew, his brother, casting a net into the sea . . . for they were fishermen. And he said to them, 'Follow me.'" So, one of the first words that Jesus essentially said to prospective followers was "Come." "[Come], follow me." In Matthew 11:28, he also says, "Come to me, all who are weary and carrying heavy burdens, and I will give you rest."

However, it's interesting to note that in addition to saying "Come," Jesus also said, "Go." He said, "Come," on one hand, and then "Go," on the other hand. He told his disciples in Luke, "Go, tell [Herod Antipas]: 'Listen, I am casting out demons and performing miracles to-day and tomorrow, and on the third day, I will finish my work." Also, he said, "Go! Go out into the road and lanes, highways and hedges, and compel people to come in, so that my house may be filled." And finally, "Go! Go make disciples of all nations . . . teaching them to observe all things which I have commanded you (Matthew 28:19–20). So, coming and going comprise two phases of one activity in the divine-human relationship. It is often said in churches or in church bulletins "Come to Worship" and "Depart to Serve." "Come," on one hand, and "Depart," on the other hand. The two action words "Worship" and "Serve" are put together in noun form to produce "Worship-Service."

The sixteenth century Protestant reformer, Martin Luther maintained that faith in God would produce good works. He agreed with the Apostle Paul that we are not saved by works. Luther's theology can, perhaps, be summed up in Paul's letter to the Romans, specifically Chapter 1:17. "The just shall live by faith." Like Matthew, there is a corollary in the Book of James: "Even so faith, if it has no works, is dead." The nineteenth century founder of the Methodist movement, John Welsey, thought that the mark of a true Christian is right practice, the sacraments rightly administered, and a person's life bearing fruit. "Bearing fruit" means "good works." So, again, Saint John 15 is relevant here. Jesus says: "My Father is glorified by this, that you bear much fruit, and become my disciples." This emphasis on service parallels Jesus' own mission statement. In Luke 4, Jesus gives his inaugural sermon before beginning his work. His sermon is based on the same text from Isaiah 61: "The Spirit of the Lord is upon me because he has anointed me to bring good news to the poor. He has sent me to bring good news to proclaim release to the captives and recovery of sight to the blind, to let the oppressed go free and proclaim the year of the Lord's favor."

When Jesus sent out the twelve disciples, He charged them: "Heal the sick, raise the dead, cleanse the lepers, cast out demons." In short, to do what He was doing. But how many of us feel inadequate? Do we sometimes think the responsibilities are too great? We may say, "I can't. The needs are too great." "What difference can I make?" Jesus shows us that one person can make a difference. He gave his life to God and encouraged his disciples to be directed by the same love of God, and to receive assistance from the Holy Spirit. His message to the disciples is also a message to us. "Live a life of Worship Service." Yes, make a joyful noise unto the Lord through songs of praise and adoration. Yes, worship the Lord with gladness and come before his presence with singing. Enter his gates with thanksgiving, and his courts with praise. Yes, give thanks to him and bless his name. Yes, come! But go! Go into the world and let your light shine, so others can see your good works and glorify God. Be a candle in the dark. Be a champion for justice. Live a life of Worship-Service. There were many men and women and who heard God's call to a life of Worship-Service. For example, Abraham was called by God in Genesis 12. God said, "Go to a land that I will show you." Deborah was called as a judge in Judges 4. Moses was called in Exodus 3 and was instructed to speak truth to power. Isaiah was called in Isaiah 6 after hearing the question: "Who will go and who shall I send?" Isaiah answered, "Here am I." Saul of Tarsus was called on the Damascus Road and Saul turned his life around from being a persecutor of Christians to being a Christian missionary. There are many other men and women who responded to God's call and who were faithful in fulfilling their callings. Space nor time permit a longer list of names but there are many others who responded to God's call and who are still responding.

In the early thirteenth century, the words of our text transformed the son of a wealthy, Italian cloth merchant who was not the most disciplined. He wasted much time and money in unwholesome activities. He attended some the best schools in Europe but was not a serious scholar. He was indifferent to the prevailing mores and customs of his day. His name was Giovanni di Bernardone but few people know him by his birth name. He was also nicknamed "Il Francesco the Frenchman" because he was easy going and lighthearted. However, the words of Matthew 10 burned in his heart and transformed him. The world knows him as Francis of Assisi or Saint Francis—the founder of the Franciscan Order. He turned to a life of reverence, poverty, and service. He trusted in God to provide for all his needs. Saint Francis did not separate worship from work. The mind and spirit of Christ were so much a part of him that his life was a continual ministry to all whom he met, even to birds. The writings of Saint Francis are similar to those of King Solomon and to those in the Westminster Catechism. King Solomon says: "Fear God and keep his commandments, for that is the whole duty of everyone" (Ecclesiastes 12:13). The Westminster Catechism says: "[Our] chief duty is to obey God and to enjoy Him forever."

God's Solution to a World of Pollution

Dr. Echol L. Nix, Sr.

"If my people, which are called by my name, shall humble themselves, and pray, and seek my face, and turn from their wicked ways; then will I hear from heaven, and will forgive their sin, and will heal their land."— II Chronicles 7:14

Throughout history we have been faced with many kinds of pollution. The air that we breathe is often contaminated with smoke, dust, grease, and grime. Contamination is found in the food that we eat and the water we drink. These products are often contaminated with germs and other various micro-organisms. While traveling up and down streets, roadways and highways of our nation, we notice paper and garbage as well as rodents and insects that have infested and polluted many residential areas.

As I survey other forms of pollution, there is one that is the most tragic of all. It has caused short-term and long-term damage to people's homes, churches, communities, and personal lives. It is spelled with a three letter word—S-I-N—and affects everybody, regardless of race, social status, gender, or geography. There have been presidents, governors, congressmen, mayors, and other prominent officials who have been impeached and moved from their respective positions because of this kind of pollution. Pastors, preachers, teachers, lawyers, principals, counselors, laymen, and rich and poor people alike have lost good positions because of this kind of pollution. Husbands and wives have started out on terrific terms and ended up on terrible terms because of this kind of pollution. Mothers, daughters, fathers, and sons have killed one another because of this kind of pollution. Alcoholics and drug addicts are in a desperate need for a quick fix because of this kind of pollution. Church memberships have started out with high numbers and now struggling to survive due to this kind of pollution. Wars, gangs, stealing, looting, and other forms of violence are on the rise because of this kind of pollution.

In biblical history we find that this pollution caused men to sweat and women to bear pain in childbirth (Genesis 3:16, 17). It caused the first murder to be committed in the Bible (Genesis 4:8). It caused the Israelites to wander in the wilderness for forty years (Numbers 14:29–35). It prevented Moses and Aaron from entering the Promised Land (Numbers 20:12). It caused Saul, the first king of Israel, to lose his connection with God (I Samuel 15:35).

It caused the second king of Israel, David, to lose his spiritual joy (Psalms 51:10–12). It caused the third king of Israel, Solomon, to worship idol gods (I Kings 11:3–9). Sin caused King Ahab to die a dreadful death (I Kings 22:34–39). Because of this kind of pollution the Northern Kingdom and Southern Kingdom were destroyed (II Kings 17 and II Kings 25, respectively).

As we have taken a bird's eye view to the secular and biblical histories of how sin causes devastation, I believe there is a solution to this world of pollution. Philosophers such as Plato, Aristotle, Socrates, Euripedes, Thales, and others might say that the answer is found in philosophical speculation while scientists might argue that science can cure all of our problems. However, the ultimate answer is not found in technological equipment like test tubes or compound microscopes. You might talk with an anthropologist, a person who studies the origins and behaviors of human beings, and he or she might point to social, cultural and historical institutions. An archaeologist who studies artifacts and remains would begin with fossils. Nevertheless, answers to the mysteries of life will not be solely found in relics. You might even wish to speak with King David who said in Psalms 55:6: "Oh that I had wings like a dove! for then would I fly away, and be at rest." However, my response is, "Don't fly David because the answer is not found in flying away."

I am reminded of a London policeman who was walking his beat on the Waterloo Bridge and spied a man about to jump. The bobby (London police are called "bobbies") managed to get to him just in time. "Come now," said the bobby, "Tell me what is the matter? Is it money?" The man said, "No." "Is it your wife?" Again there was a negative reply. "Well, what is it then?" "I'm worried about the condition of the world," admitted the man. "Oh, come now," replied the bobby reassuringly. "It can't be as bad as all that. Walk up and down the bridge with me and let's talk it over." And so the two men took a walk, discussing the world's problems for about an hour, and then they both jumped over the bridge.

The solution to this pollution comes back to the scripture: "If my people who are called by my name shall humble themselves, and pray, seek my face, and turn from their wicked ways; then will I hear from heaven, and will forgive their sin, and heal their land" (II Chronicles 7:14). The context and setting of the Scripture is at the dedication of the Temple that Solomon built. The Scripture is based on God's covenant with Solomon concerning the land and the people at that time. God is talking to Solomon about the nation of Israel and Israel was made up of twelve tribes. In order from the oldest to the youngest, the tribes were (as first recorded in Genesis): Reuben, Simeon, Levi, Judah, Dan, Naphtali, Gad, Asher, Issachar, Zebulun, Joseph, and Benjamin. Because Joseph was not a tribe, Ephraim and Manasseh, Joseph's sons were the substituted tribes for him. Today the people of Israel are scattered throughout the world and peace is still a constant goal due to religious strife, social divisions and violence.

In making contemporary applications, there is a message in the text for you and for me. It would be unwise to dismiss this message just because it was written perhaps in the fourth or fifth century B.C.E. I feel that it is a formula for our time. "My people" means "God's people" and "God's people" includes the Christian church or "the body of Christ." These are the ones who have accepted Jesus as their personal Savior. The Bible says, "Who gave himself for us, that he might redeem us from all iniquity, and purify unto himself a peculiar people, zealous of good works" (Titus 2:14). In this scriptural text, the writer refers to four things (or we could say four variables) which equal the whole. Mathematically, each one could be considered "1x." So, $1x + 1x + 1x + 1x = 4x$, which is God's solution. Breaking it down to the least common denominator, the first "1x" means "humility"; the second "1x" means "prayer"; the third "1x" means "to seek God"; and the fourth "1x" means "to turn around." This equals God's solution. Let's briefly examine the first "1x."

Humility is humbling yourself before God. This is being able to control thoughts and actions by surrendering your own selfish desires. Humility is being able to stop, look, and listen before proceeding or jumping to conclusions. Humility is making sure you are right before moving forward. All of us need humility. Dr. Martin Luther King,

Jr. stated in his book, *Strength to Love*:

> The hardhearted person never truly loves. He en-
> gages in a crass utilitarianism which values other people
> mainly according to their usefulness to him. He never
> experiences the beauty of friendship, because he is too
> cold to feel affection for another and is too self-centered
> to share another's joy and sorrow. He is an island that is
> isolated. There is no outpouring of love that links him
> with the mainland of humanity.[6]

Humility is having a tender heart full of love and compassion for others. Jesus said in Saint Luke 14:11, "For whosoever exalteth himself shall be abased; and he that humbleth
himself shall be exalted." Without humility, humans are
like a bear making tracks but not getting anywhere. We
are like a bird trying to fly without wings. We are like a
truck traveling the interstate without a driver.

Second, before we can solve the pollution of sin, we
need the next "1x" which is prayer. Prayer is a sincere
plea to God. It is humanity's spiritual desire, motivated
by a hunger and thirst for God. Prayer is a wish turned
upward. An anonymous poet wrote:

> Prayer is the soul's sincere desire, uttered or unex-
> pressed; The motion of hidden fire that trembles in the
> breast; Prayer is the simplest form of speech that infant

---

6   Dr. Martin Luther, King, Jr., *Strength to Love* (Philadelphia, Pennsyl-
vania: Fortress Press, 1963), 17.

lips can try; Prayer—the sublimest strains that reach the majesty on high; Prayer is the contrite sinner's voice. Returning from his ways, While angels in their songs rejoice, and say, "Behold, he prays; Prayer is the Christian's vital breath, The Christian's native air, His watchword at the gate of death; He enters Heaven with prayer.

Personally, I believe that there is power in prayer. God granted Hannah her wish for a son. He gave her Samuel who became a priest, prophet, and judge. God also blessed her to have other children. Elijah prayed on Mount Carmel and fire came down from Heaven. Daniel's prayer was answered in the lion's den. Paul and Silas' prayers were answered in the Philippian jail. Charles Spurgeon, one of the world's greatest preachers said: "Prayer pulls the cord which rings the bell in the ears of God." He further said, "So many pull the cord in a weak way; others just occasionally; while others continue with all their might to pull the cord and ring the bells of promise in the ears of God."

The third "1x" is to seek God. Too many of us seek after everything except the right thing. We seek adventure by playing dangerous sports. We seek beauty by going to the beautician and barber and putting on lip stick, powder, face creams, perfumes, or colognes. We seek music by listening to jazz, country, pop, rock, soul, and gospel. We seek pleasure by lovemaking, going to the race tracks, casinos, playing bingo and other card games, shooting pool, dancing, or exercising. There is nothing wrong with being a seeker but we should seek and study God's Word. Jesus was a seeker. He stated in Saint Luke 19:10: "For the Son of man is come to seek and to save that which was lost." Paul told Timothy, "Study to shew thyself approved unto God, a workman that needeth not to be ashamed, rightly dividing the word of truth" (II Timothy 2:15). Studying is like putting money in the bank. If you don't put any in, you won't get any out. If you study you will be able to watch and understand God's television.

God's television is broken up into sixty-six channels on two networks. There are 39 on Network One and 27 on Network Two. On Network One—The Old Testament— you will find: Genesis, Exodus, Leviticus, Numbers, Deuteronomy, Joshua, Judges, Ruth, I Samuel, II Samuel, I Kings, II Kings, I Chronicles, II Chronicles, Ezra, Nehemiah, Esther, Job, Psalms, Proverbs, Ecclesiastes, Song of Solomon, Isaiah, Jeremiah, Lamentations, Ezekiel, Daniel, Hosea, Joel, Amos, Obadiah, Jonah, Micah, Nahum, Habakkuk, Zephaniah, Haggai, Zechariah, Malachi.

On Network Two—The New Testament—you will find: Matthew, Mark, Luke, John, Acts, Romans, I Corinthians, II Corinthians, Galatians, Ephesians, Philippians, Colossians, I Thessalonians, II Thessalonians, I Timothy, II Timothy, Titus, Philemon, Hebrews, James, I Peter, II Peter, I John, II John, III John, Jude, and Revelation. There were forty or more inspired writers who wrote the bible. The Bible is given different and specific names by its writers. Some include: "The Scripture" (Mark 15:28), "The Promises" (Romans 9:4), "The Oracles of God" (Romans 3:2; Hebrews 5:12), "The Book of the Lord" (Isaiah 34:16), "The Sword of the Spirit" (Ephesians 6:17), "The First and Second Covenant" (Hebrews 8:7), "The Word of Christ" (Colossians 3:16), "The Word of Faith" (Romans 10:8), and "The Word of Righteousness" (Hebrews 5:13).

When you seek God's Word, you can find many good stories in the Bible. If you read carefully you can watch some of these on God's television set. On God's television, you can watch a story called *Highway to Heaven* on the Gospel of John chapter 14:6 when Jesus told us how to get to Heaven. In this episode, he claims: "I am the way, the truth, and the life: no man cometh unto the Father, but by me." If you are a sports fan, turn your television set to Genesis chapter 32:24 and look at a *Championship Wrestling* match. In this episode, Jacob wrestled with an angel all night long. Personally, I would say that Jacob lost the fight but won the match. His name was changed from "Jacob" to "Israel."

On God's television, you can also watch *Divorce Court* on the Gospel of Mark chapter 10:9. In this episode, Jesus said: "What therefore God hath joined together, let no man put asunder." If you want to seek God's word, watch *The Edge of Night*. Saint John chapter 3:1–3 records a man of the Pharisees named Nicodemus, a ruler of the Jews. He came to Jesus by night and said: "Rabbi, we know that thou art a teacher come from God: for no man can do these miracles that thou doest, except God be with him." Jesus answered him "Verily, verily, I say unto thee, Except a man be born again, he cannot see the kingdom of God." If you want to see a show called *Amen* you can see it in the Gospel of Matthew, chapter 6:9–10. Here, Jesus showed His disciples how to pray. He said: "After this manner therefore pray ye: Our Father which art in heaven, Hallowed be thy name. Thy kingdom come, Thy will be done in earth, as it is in heaven." You can also find a show called *The Family Feud* on God's television. "And the man said, 'The woman whom thou gavest to be with me, she gave me of the tree, and I did eat.' And the Lord God said unto the woman, 'What is this that thou hast done? And the woman said, 'The serpent beguiled me, and I did eat" (Genesis 3:12–13). If you want to watch *Face the Nation*, just turn on your television set to Joshua chapter 24:15. In this dramatic episode, Joshua tells Israel: "Choose ye this day whom ye will serve . . . but as for me and my house, we will serve the Lord."

Our fourth "1x" that is needed to solve the problem of pollution is to turn around. Many of us need to turn around. We need to stop and make a 360° commitment—a complete circle which represents a whole. According to the Gestalt theory in psychology, the whole is greater than its parts. Yes, we must take a self-inventory and see ourselves going in the wrong direction. We must be able to perceive a spiritual blockade and be knowledgeable of the fact that a change in direction is needed. In order to turn around, a change is needed on the inside before there could be a change on the outside. It happened to Peter just a little before Pentecost. It happened to the woman at Jacob's well. It happened to James and John down by the shores of Galilee. It happened to Isaiah in the year that King Uzziah died. It happened to Thomas after the resurrection. It happened to Zacchaeus after coming down the sycamore tree. It happened to blind Bartimaeus near Jericho. It happened to the old woman who had spent all that she had. It happened to Paul on the Damascus Road.

Yes, it is possible for all of us to turn around. God's will is not for anybody to perish, but for all to have an abundant life. After suffering many perverse people and sinful generations, God eventually grew tired of human wickedness. After prophecies had been given to the Hebrew nation and messages addressed primarily to the post-exilic Jews after the temple had been destroyed and rebuilt, the Lord's anger was kindled against His people. Finally, after the prophet Malachi proclaimed the Day of Judgment upon the children of Israel during the last half of the fifth century B.C.E., the Lord rebuked the entire nation for their apostasy and rebellion. For four hundred years no one heard a word from the Lord.

However, using my imagination I see the Omnipotent, Omnipresent, and Omniscient God searching all over heaven and earth. Perhaps, He looked at majestic angels such as Michael, Raphael, and Gabriel. He concluded, however, that they were not worthy to redeem humanity of its sins and be the moral exemplar or archetype for faithful followers. So, God considered Abraham, who was "the father of many nations," but Abraham's flaw was telling Abimelech, king of Gerar, and Pharaoh the king of Egypt, that Sarah was his sister and not his wife. Further, God examined Jacob. Jacob was the father of the twelve tribes of Israel, but he stole his brother Esau's birthright. What about the famous lawgiver and liberator Moses? Moses' problem was disobedience. What about of David, a man after God's own heart? David was an adulterer. Was Solomon worthy? Solomon was the king who asked for wisdom and understanding, but Solomon's affairs resulted in idol worship. God analyzed the lives of all the priests, including Aaron, Eleazar, Eli, all the judges from Othniel to Samuel; all the kings who ruled in Israel and Judah—nineteen from the Northern Kingdom and twenty from the Southern Kingdom, as well as those representing other nations. Reviewing the profiles of the major prophets—Isaiah, Jeremiah, Ezekiel, and Daniel—God was disappointed because they would ultimately prove unworthy of such a task.

Moreover, God ruled out the minor prophets—Hosea, Joel, Amos, Obadiah, Jonah, Micah, Nahum, Habakkuk, Zephaniah, Haggai, Zechariah, and Malachi. They, too, were in need of redemption. I imagine God turned to Jesus and said: "I've searched all over and can't find anybody like you." I imagine Jesus replied: "If it is your will, give me a physical body, including a head with brain organs such as a cerebrum, cerebellum, and medulla oblongata." Jesus probably asked for some hands to perform miracles and magnify God's name through the power to heal. He probably asked for feet so He could walk around the shores of Galilee and call disciples who would become "fishers of men." Then, He needed a heart full of love, love that picks those up who have fallen down by the wayside; a love that laughs when others are crying; a love that looks up when others are looking down; a love that pays off and is not bankrupt; a love that will stay with you when others forsake you.

Also, Jesus probably said that He would leave the throne of Glory, travel through forty-two generations (from Abraham to David were fourteen generations, from David to the carrying away into Babylon were fourteen generations, and from the carrying away into Babylon to the coming of Christ were 14 generations). He then would live on Earth for thirty-three and a half years, heal the sick, raise the dead, give sight to the blind, be crucified on a Roman cross, and be resurrected on the third day morning. All who believe within their hearts that He died and rose again can be saved. Through Christ all are given the opportunity to turn around. Saint John 3:16 states: "For God so loved the world, that he gave his only begotten Son, that whosoever believeth in him should not perish, but have everlasting life." God's solution to a world of pollution is: (1) humility, (2) prayer, (3) seek

God, and (4) turn around. An anonymous writer issues the following invitation:

COME TO JESUS

Come to Jesus, Come to Jesus, Come to Jesus just now;
Just now, come to Jesus, Come to Jesus, just now.

He will save you, He will save you, He will save you, just
    now;
Just now, He will save you, He will save you, just now.

Important Signs that Can Direct You to the King's Highway

Dr. Echol L. Nix, Sr.

"And a highway shall be there, and a way, and it shall be called The Way of Holiness; the unclean shall not pass over it; but it shall be for those: the wayfaring men, though fools, shall not err therein."— Isaiah 35:8

As we travel around the United States, whether north, south, east, or west there are certain times when we find ourselves traveling on the wrong road. Sometimes we may take the wrong exit. Sometimes we take a right turn when we should have taken a left turn. Other times regardless of the way we turn, a situation may be depressing, messy and confusing. However, despite chaos, tragedy, and confusion, I believe that there are certain signs that can lead us to a safe destination. I don't believe that all signs are blown down and washed away in a sea of moral decay. I must hold to the truth and faith that all rules and regulations are not caught up in the whirlwinds, tornados, and hurricanes of change. I am convinced that there are certain signs that can help keep us on a safe course and in the right direction. However, throughout this sermon, my analysis will be limited to six signs that are significant in leading us to a very significant destination—the King's Highway.

The first sign on this long and less traveled journey is the Stop sign. This sign often stands out in the mind of many because it is red and white. It gets your attention. I remember when my wife used to wear her red and white outfits when we were dating—she would catch my attention based on her attractiveness. The stop sign has the same effect. It means to make a complete stop, check all ways, and go when safe to proceed. However, before entering onto the King's Highway, we must adhere to this sign to make a complete stop. In terms of signs, there could be things that we are doing that need to be stopped and dropped. Whatever we are doing against the will of God must be stopped. So, let us never forget to adhere to the Stop sign.

The second sign we need to recognize before traveling the King's Highway is the Yield sign. When driving, many people disregard the Yield sign. The sign is important because it allows others the right of way to go before you can proceed. It teaches us to have respect for others. It enforces the commonly stated Golden Rule: "Do unto others as you would have them do unto you." The Yield sign also teaches patience. Patience is a wonderful virtue. The classical understanding of patience is "to stand still" when you desire to go forward. Isaiah 40:31 reminds us that "they that wait who upon the Lord shall renew their strength; they shall mount up with wings as eagles; they shall run, and not be weary; and they shall walk, and not faint." No discipline can be imagined more severe for the average, restless person than patience. A patient person is rare. Job has been called the most patient of men. Someone has suggested that there are three stages in the exercise of patience. First it is simply submission to the Will of God. Second, it expresses itself in persistent endurance. Third, it is the quality of your faith in God. It was this kind of faith and patience exemplified by the Hebrew boys in the hot, fiery furnace when they proclaimed, "My God is able" (Daniel 3). It is this type of patience and faith that William Ernest Henley describes in his poem "Invictus":

> Out of the night that covers me,
> Black as the Pit from pole to pole,
> I thank whatever gods may be
> For my unconquerable soul.
>
> In the fell clutch of circumstance
> I have not winced nor cried aloud.
> Under the bludgeoning of chance

My head is bloody, but unbowed.

Beyond this place of wrath and tears
Looms but the Horror of the shade,
And yet the menace of the years
Finds, and shall find, me afraid.

It matters not how strait the gate,
How charged with punishments the scroll,
I am the master of my fate:
I am the captain of my soul.

So it is important for us to observe the Yield sign.

Our third sign that we need to be aware of before entering onto the King's Highway is the "Do Not Enter" sign. It is very important that we obey this sign. This sign teaches us self-control. It will keep you from having a head-on collision or driving on the wrong side of the road. Many men and women have died because of failing to heed the "Do Not Enter" sign. It is mandatory that we obey this particular sign. Many times Satan has a way to enter our minds at our weakest point. I know he can do this because Satan got into my mind when I was in high school and college and made me think I was the "Love Man," as it related to the ladies and being the most popular on campus. However, it took many years later for me to find out that Jesus is the real "Love Man." Satan even tried to enter Jesus' mind. He told Jesus, "'If thou be the Son of God, command that these stones be made bread.' But he [Jesus] answered and said, 'It is written, Man shall not live by bread alone, but by every word that proceedeth out of the mouth of God'" (Matthew 4:3–4). An example in the Bible of not adhering to God's "Do Not Enter" sign is King Saul and as a result he was rejected by God after becoming the first king of Israel. The "Do Not Enter" sign of disobedience caused Moses in the Old Testament not to enter the Promised Land. Therefore, I highly encourage you not to forget the "Do Not Enter" sign.

A significant sign on our journey as well is the "No Passing Zone" sign. With this sign, we need to know when to hold them and when to roll them. Hold them and roll them meaning our words and actions. Sometimes we may be in a situation that tests our patience and tolerance, but similar to the "No Passing Zone" sign, we must remain calm, cool, and collected if we are to reach our destination safely. Remember this line from the relevant song, "I'm so glad, troubles doesn't last always." Please be mindful of the "No Passing Zone" sign.

Our fifth sign which needs to be recognized is the Speed sign. We might as well face it, many of us are driving too fast or too slow. Either one can be just as dangerous as the other. As we prepare to travel the King's Highway, let us observe the Speed sign. Try not to speed through these days and run the risk of burning up and burning out. You will miss too much of the tourist attractions and beautiful scenery along life's highway when you speed through life.

You will not get a chance to appreciate all that mother nature has to offer. There is also a danger of getting a ticket, being put in jail, getting killed, or killing somebody else. One of my current students called me recently and said that he would not be able to attend class because he had to conduct a funeral where he was burying two of his church members. The members were a father and son who had been killed in a vehicle crash on an interstate outside of Birmingham, AL.

Remember what Matthew 7:13–14 says: "Enter ye in at the strait gate: for wide is the gate, and broad is the way, that leadeth to destruction, and many there be which go in thereat: Because strait is the gate, and narrow is the way, which leadeth unto life, and few there be that find it." I highly recommend you not to forget the Speed sign.

The last sign I will mention in this sermon is the Blue sign. This particular sign indicates service such as a rest area, hospital, food restaurants, or lodging. Rest is important when driving because you could go into a state of highway hypnosis or velocitization. Either state is similar to that of a deep sleep and a loss of direction. You become completely unaware due to a loss of consciousness. Rest, however, could eliminate many of these problems. It has been recommended by medical authority for the body to get at least eight hours of rest each night. Humans need rest in order to function properly. Rest serves as a therapeutic treatment for the body and mind. Jesus knew this when He stated in Matthew 11:28: "Come unto me, all ye that labour and are heavy laden, and I will give you rest." I highly recommend you to adhere and to respect the Blue sign.

Nevertheless, as you travel the King's Highway, please carry a special friend with you just as you might ordinarily drive with someone for companionship, protection or driving and roadside assistance. While driving, you just don't know what might happen. Your cell phone signal might get weak. People might try to highjack you. There could be car problems, accidents, sickness, or even death. On the King's Highway, the friend I recommend is Jesus Christ who will stick closer than a brother. A song writer summed this relationship with these words: "What a friend we have in Jesus. All our sins and grieves to bear! What a privilege to carry everything to God in prayer! O what peace we often forfeit, O what needless pain we bear, all because we do not carry, everything to God in prayer." Personally, I have found Jesus Christ to be that friend.

During my many years teaching Driver Education and traffic safety, I developed procedures to help beginning students: They are as follows:

Procedures for Pre-Driving Checks

1. Check condition of vehicle (tires, lights, etc.).

2. Check around the vehicle.

3. Check intended path of travel.

Procedures for Starting the Car

1. Close and lock doors.

2. Adjust seat and mirrors.

3. Fasten seatbelt.

4. Make sure the car is in park.

5. Make sure parking brake is on.

6. Put key in switch.

7. Cover brake, turn switch, start car, release key and get proper air.

Procedures for Moving the Car

1. Continue to hold foot on brake.

2. Put car in desired gear.

3. Release parking brake.

4. Check traffic.

5. Signal.

6. Check traffic over left and right shoulders.

7. Take foot off brake.

8. Apply gas pedal gently.

The last procedure is to apply the gas pedal gently. As you apply the gas, I keep moving in the right direction. The right direction could start with "Belief Boulevard."

Paul writes: "If thou shalt confess with thy mouth the Lord Jesus, and shalt believe in thine heart that God hath raised him from the dead, thou shalt be saved. For with the heart man believeth unto righteousness; and with thy mouth confession is made unto salvation." From there you may proceed onto the "Bridge of Faith" which is over troubled water. Hebrews 11:1 states: "Now faith is the substance of things hoped for, the evidence of things not seen." I heard a songwriter say, "Trouble in my way, I have to cry sometimes. I lay awake at night, but that's alright, I know that Jesus will fix it afterwhile."

After traveling "Trinity Lane" while reflecting on the Father, Son, and Holy Spirit, exit on "Grace Boulevard." God's grace is sufficient. Then, make a turn on "Gospel Lane" where you will learn much about the good news of Jesus Christ. Keep straight and make a right on "Prayer Road" because there is power in prayer. For example, the prayer of Elijah brought fire from Heaven (I Kings 18). Daniel's prayer was heard in the Lion's Den (Daniel 6:16–28). James 5:16 states: "The effectual fervent prayer of a righteous man availeth much." After leaving "Prayer Road," keep straight and yield not to the traffic on "Temptation Avenue." You must avoid "Sin Street." The only way to avoid "Sin Street" is to keep straight. You might experience slower traffic in the right lane but keep going straight. You might travel down "Persecution Boulevard," but keep going straight. You might experience a "Trial and Tribulation Detour" but keep going straight. You might experience the toll roads of "being talked about," but keep going straight. Men and women at work might be a part of the road's problem, but keep straight. Keep straight until there is no need for the sun. Keep straight until there are no more seas. Keep straight until the sun sets and the day is done. Keep straight until you get to a sign that says, "Well done, thou good and faithful servant . . . Enter into the joy of the Lord" (Matthew 25:21). Keep straight until the battle is fought and the victory is won. The final procedures from the aforementioned list are:

Procedures for Parking the Car

1. Continue to hold foot on brake.
2. Apply parking brake.
3. Put car in park.
4. Turn switch off and take key out of switch.
5. Take foot off brake.
6. Make sure lights are off.
7. Unfasten seatbelts.
8. Secure all windows and doors with the exception of exit.
9. Get out on curbside, if possible, and lock exit door with key in your hand.

Once you park, you have completed the journey. A traditional hymn says, "He'll Understand and Say 'Well Done.'"

Oh when I come to the end of my journey
Weary of life and the battle is won
Carrying the staff and the cross of redemption
He'll understand and say well done.
Misunderstood, yes the Saviour of sinners
Died on the cross, he was God's only son
But he knew well that his father in heaven
Would understand and say well done

Oh hear him calling his father in heaven
"Not my will Lord but thine be done."

And when I come to the end of my journey
Weary of life and the battle is won
Caring the staff and the cross of redemption
He'll understand and say, "Well done."

The Marks of a Champion

Dr. Echol L. Nix, Sr.

"I press toward the mark for the prize of the high calling of God in Christ Jesus." — Philippians 3:14

The apostle Paul wrote this text. He was often called "the great apostle to the Gentiles." Paul was born in Tarsus, the chief city of Cilicia. He was from the tribe of Benjamin. Gamaliel, one of the most learned and distinguished rabbis of the day was his teacher. Paul was on his way to persecute Christians when he met Jesus on the Damascus Road. After his traumatic experience on the Damascus Road, his whole life was changed and he was never the same. His conversion experience is recorded in the Book of Acts, Chapter 9.

After his conversion experience, he stopped hating Christians and began to call them "my beloved brothers and sisters." This is why Paul was able to later write in 2 Corinthians 5:17: "Therefore if any man be in Christ, he is a new creature: old things are passed away; behold, all things are become new." The epistle to the Philippians is one of four epistles that Paul wrote while in prison. The other prison epistles are Ephesians, Colossians, and Philemon. A main theme of Philippians is persistence in the face of opposition and even the threat of death. Paul was an example of steadfast courage and joy in the midst of harsh circumstances. He encouraged the Philipians in his day. I encourage Christians today around the world to press toward the mark for the prize of the high calling of God in Christ Jesus.

In order to press for the prize, I highly recommend three steps. They are: (1) Aim High, (2) Move In, and (3) Hit Hard.

"Aim high" means to look upward. As you look up, keep your eyes on God. Rain, wind, snow, hail, or high water—keep your focus on God. He is omniscient, meaning "all knowing;" He is omnipotent, meaning "all powerful"; He is omnipresent, meaning "everywhere." By "aiming high" you will be able to get the big picture. You can predict your anticipation, decide on your path, and execute your direction. The concept of "aiming high" reminds me of the story about a boy who went hunting with a shot gun. His dream was to return with the largest game possible. He looked up in a tree and saw a squirrel and looked a little higher and saw a wild turkey. The boy positioned himself and shot at the turkey. The buck shots scattered and hit the squirrel. A limb was shot off the tree and hit a running deer and broke its neck. The discharge from the gun was so strong that it knocked the boy into the pond.

As the boy recovered from the incident, he got up and noticed that his pockets were also full of fish. By aiming high, the boy hit the turkey, squirrel and deer. In addition to hitting all three of them, he ended up with more than expected—a pocket full of fish. C. W. Longenecker wrote in his poem "The Victor":

> If you think you're beaten, you are;
> If you think that you dare not, you don't;
> If you'd like to win, but think you can't,
> It's almost for sure you won't.
>
> If you think you'll lose, you've lost;
> For out in the world you'll find
> Success begins with a fellow's will.
> It's all in the state of mind.
>
> If you think you're outclassed, you are;
> You've got to think high to rise;
> You've got to be sure of yourself before
> You can ever win a prize.
>
> Life's battle don't always go
> To the stronger or faster man;
> But sooner or later the man who wins
> Is the man who thinks he can.

Second, in order to win the prize I highly recommend

that you "move in." One must have faith and courage in order to "move in." According to Hebrews 11:1, Faith is "the substance of things hoped for, the evidence of things not seen." Faith is believing that you can when the world says "you cannot." Faith is not only "talking the talk" but also "walking the walk of being a faithful believer."

Before retiring as a Master Teacher in Driver's Education for the state of Alabama, my high school and college students often asked me to share with them a few motivational quotes. The following quotations have been very helpful to me as well to them. Hopefully, they will be helpful to you, too.

> "Do a job so well that no man living, dead or yet to be born could do it any better." — Dr. Benjamin E. Mays

> "I would rather die and go to hell by choice than to stumble into heaven by following the crowd." — Dr. Benjamin E. Mays

> "It must be borne in mind that the tragedy of life doesn't lie in not reaching your goal; the tragedy lies in having no goals to reach." — Dr. Benjamin E. Mays

> "It is not how big the dog in the fight but how much fight in the dog." — Author Unknown

> "A fool will get lost and ask for directions, but a wise man asks for directions before getting lost." — Pastor Johnny Carter

"If you fail to plan, you plan to fail." — Author Unknown

"It is not where you line up but where you wind up." — Rev. Dr. Echol L. Nix, Sr.

"It is of paramount importance not just for you to get it good but for you to get it real, real, real good." — Rev. Dr. Echol L. Nix, Sr.

"Before you jump into the water, check the depth and prepare to dive." — Rev. Dr. Echol L. Nix, Sr.

"It takes a small man who will make others look bad in order to make himself look good." — Rev. Dr. Echol L. Nix, Sr.

"It's not a black or white thing, but it's the right thing." — Rev. Dr. Echol L. Nix, Sr.

"Short cuts bring scars." — Rev. Dr. Echol L. Nix, Sr.

"Experience is a combination of hell and frustration mixed with determination." — Rev. Dr. Echol L. Nix, Sr.

"Love is the only force capable of transforming an enemy into a friend." — Dr. Martin Luther King, Jr.

"We must live together as brothers or perish together as fools." — Dr. Martin Luther King, Jr.

"Life has two rules: Number 1, never quit; Number 2, always remember rule Number 1." — Duke Ellington

"If you an out-think a man, you can beat him." — Dr. Tommy Frederick

"I don't know the key to success, but the key to failure is trying to please everybody." — Dr. William (Bill) Cosby

"Failure can be divided into those who thought and never did and those who did and never thought." — Rev. W. A. Nance

"Be nice to folks on your way up because you might meet them on your way back down." — Jimmy Durnate

"When life knocks you down, try to fall on your back because if you can look up, then you can get up." — Les Brown

"Some things in life are designed to make you fail but when you are in Christ you will always prevail." Elder Larry Lewis, Sr.

"Life is filled with ups and downs, problems and folks who make you frown; but, if you are willing to go the extra mile, your frown will become a smile." — Elder Larry Lewis, Sr.

"Son, remember to be yourself." — Mrs. Rebethar L. Nix (My mother)

As you continue to press toward the prize of the high calling never forget to hit hard. It takes power and determination to hit hard. Winston Churchhill once stated: "Never, ever, ever, ever, ever give up." History has recorded many hard hitting champions. The Apostle Paul was one when he wrote: "I can do all things through Christ which strengthens me." Moses was another who affirmed: "Stand still and see the salvation of the Lord." Joshua declared: "As for me and my house we will serve the Lord." Job exclaimed: "Though he slays me, yet will I trust in him." Joseph proclaimed: "You meant it for evil, but God meant it for good." David acknowledged, "The Lord is my Shepherd, I shall not want." Solomon concluded: "Let us hear the conclusion of the whole matter: Fear God, and keep His commandment: for this is the whole duty of man."

Furthermore, as a hard hitter, remember to read the bible. You should read it prayerfully, meditatively, seriously, industriously, and spiritually. It is the score keeper's time clock, the teacher's lesson plan, the traveler's road map, the pilgrim's staff, the lexicographer's lexicon, the pilot's compass, the Christian's charter, the architect's blue print, and the poet's metaphor. Although the liberal arts and sciences can and should be studied, I also encourage you to consider Matthew 6:33: "Seek ye first the Kingdom of God and His righteousness; and all these things shall be added unto you." It's nothing wrong with learning many academic disciplines, but it's also important to know about God's plan for salvation. Paul writes in Romans 10:9: "If thou shalt confess with thy mouth the Lord Jesus, and shalt believe in thine heart that God hath raised him from the dead, thou shalt be saved." It's great to study theological and philosophical writings from Søren Kierkegaard, Karl Barth, Martin Luther, John Calvin, Walter Rauschenbush, Paul Tillich,

Rudolf Bultmann, Reinhold Niebuhr, Dietrich Bonhoeffer, James Cone, Thomas Aquinas and others. However, it's better if your life could reflect those writings and to exemplify the words of Matthew 5:16: "Let your light so shine before men, that they may see your good works, and glorify your Father which is in heaven."

In addition to studying educational materials in secular schools, I think it's good to supplement those studies with Paul's admonition in 2 Timothy 2:15, "Study to shew thyself approved unto God, a workman that needeth not to be ashamed, rightly dividing the word of truth."

In closing, please remember that a true champion must (1) Aim High, (2) Move In, and (3) Hit Hard. I hope this will be your motivation to press toward the mark of the high calling which is in Jesus Christ. The prize is Jesus Christ. Personally, I know Him as:

A: All Powerful (St. Matthew 28:18)

B: Bread of Life (St. John 6:35; 6:48)

C: Comforter (St. Matthew 5:4)

D: Deliverer (Romans 11:26)

E: Everlasting Father (Isaiah 9:6)

F: Faithful Witness (Revelation 1:5)

G: Good Shepherd (St. John 10:11, 14)

H: Holy One (Acts 3:14)

I: I Am (St. John 8:58)

J: Just (Acts 7:52)

K: King of kings (I Timothy 6:15; Rev. 19:16)

L: Lord of lords (Revelation 19:16)

M: Morning Star (Revelation 22:16)

N: Nazarene (St. Matthew 2:23)

O: Our Protection (II Thessalonians 3:3)

P: Prince of Peace (Isaiah 9:6)

Q: Quickening (life-giving) Spirit (I Corinthians 15:45)

R: Righteous One (Acts 7:52; I John 2:1)

S: Savior (Ephesians 5:23; Titus 1:4; 3:6; II Peter 2:20)

T: Truth (John 1:14; 14:6)

U: Unspeakable Gift (II Corinthians 9:15)

V: Vine (St. John 15:51)

W: Wonderful Counselor (Isaiah 9:6)

X: X-Ray (Psalm 139:1)

Y: Yearning (Psalm 42:1–2)

Z: Zenith of MY LIFE (Genesis 14:20)

From Generation to Generation

DR. ECHOL L. NIX, JR.

"My child, do not forget my teaching, but let your heart keep my commandments, for length of days and years of life and abundant welfare they will give you." — Proverbs 3:1–2, RSV

The words of this text were written by Solomon. He reigned as king of Israel for forty years and was responsible for building the first Temple in Jerusalem. Solomon was so impressive, the queen of Sheba visited his palace and returned saying: "The half has not even been told." In Matthew 6:29, Jesus made reference to Solomon's glory: "Even Solomon in all his glory was not arrayed like one of these," referring to the natural beauty of the lilies of the field. Solomon's vast building program and his patronage of the arts were all regarded with awe by visitors from far and near. In addition to possessing wealth, Solomon was famous for his wisdom. While Israel was united, it moved from a loose confederation of tribes to being a political and economic power, among other nations. Saul was the first king and David was the second king during the time of Israel's united kingdom. David's leadership is historically celebrated and he was considered a man after God's own heart.

Shortly before David's death, the united kingdom began to slip out of control due to the revolt of Edom and Syria. Although Solomon was not a military leader like his father, he used political tactics and international diplomacy to carry out and stabilize the policies David initiated. The political success during David's time was continued during Solomon's administration. Egypt was not as strong as Israel and Assyria would not be a threat for almost a century later. Further, Israel controlled other smaller nations through military action or commercial treaty. As a result, Israel was feared by others but Solomon emphasized the "fear of the Lord." Proverbs 9:10 says, "The fear of the Lord is the beginning of wisdom." "Fear" in this context means "a deep desire to please God," "an intense reverence" "to be righteous," and "to not disappoint God in anyway." Solomon writes these words and passes them on from one generation to another. These are helpful suggestions on how to be prosperous, successful, and virtuous. He writes in Proverbs 15:1 that "a soft answer turns away wrath, but a harsh word stirs up anger." In Proverbs 16:18, he offers another wise thought: "Pride goes before destruction and a haughty spirit before a fall."

The entire book of Proverbs has insights whereby a young person might learn to cope with the challenges of life. According to the biblical scholar Bruce Metzger, the book has themes that relate to ethical conduct and judgments. "Some sayings are observations, but more often than not, they are moral principles. The underlying principle is: 'The fear of the Lord is the beginning of wisdom.'" Solomon's writings were passed down as wise sayings for generations to use and to apply. However, such writings are not unique to Solomon. In many households, there are proverbs, aphorisms, or folklore that can also be considered "wisdom literature." Some include: "What goes around, comes around." "You can take a mule to a well but you can't make him drink." "What's done in the dark will come to the light." Every closed-eye is not sleeping and every good-bye is not gone." "Birds of a feather, flock together." "Misery loves company." There are many more that are culturally specific and personally meaningful.

Solomon addresses his own people with the words of the text and tells them that if they obey, they will be blessed. The Hebrews thought that obedience to God resulted in blessings and disobedience resulted in curses. This is known as "the doctrine of retribution." In Judaism, the Shema, which Jews are supposed to recite twice daily, says: "Hear O Israel, the Lord our God is One and you shall love the Lord your God with all your soul, heart and ming." There is a vertical relationship between an individual and God and a horizontal relationship between individuals. I John 4:20 states: "For those who do not love a brother or sister whom they have seen cannot love God whom they have not seen.

Christian discipleship requires certain obligations to God, to ourselves, and to society. The Book of Proverbs explains the nature of reality and the purpose of life. First of all, we should glorify God. Second, we must make a decent living for ourselves, and third, we should strive to live in harmony with each other. The mere fact that God created us and created the world means that there is a priority on creation. Genesis 1:1 starts: "In the beginning, God created . . ." It is often said: "Who we are is God's gift to us and what we become is our gift to God." So life is important but what we make of our lives is equally important. Life is short and missed opportunities are not easily recaptured. Have you done your best? Have you taken time to call or to encourage someone in need? If not now, when? Tomorrow is not promised. There is no guarantee that any of us will be here next week or next year.

Life is fleeting and regardless of how long life lasts, it's still not long. An anonymous writer said: "I expect to pass through this world but once. Any good I can do, or any kindness that I can show, let me do it now, for I shall not pass this way again." What difference does it make that we are here? How is the world better because we were born? What does it matter that we are living in the third millennium of the common era? Is the world any more friendly? Any more just? Has knowledge been advanced because of our contributions in the fields of technology, science, medicine, and industry? Have schools and social organizations flourished because we have supported them or taken an interest in their activities and sponsored programs? Is the environment sustained because we are working to control and eliminate pollution and dangerous contaminants that affect the earth, land resources, water, plants, and animals? Are our neighborhoods any more safe from crime, drugs, and violence because we have taken a stand against everything that poses a threat to the peace and tranquility of our communities? Do our jobs create an atmosphere of professionalism and cordiality because we are a part of the team? Is our presence and witness felt by people we come in contact with in the public square or marketplace? Are churches and other social organizations financially stable because of good stewardship and accounting practices? Are educational institutions producing outstanding students based on standards of excellence and through recruitment efforts of alumni? These are some of the reasons why we are here but how are you making the world a better place? Jesus taught: "To whom much is given, much is required" (Luke 12:48). How are you "serving this present age" (to quote the hymn of Isaac Watts)? What are you passing on to the next generation? What values are you inculcating in the lives of our youth? What kind of moral example and legacy are you leaving to those who follow?

It's not enough to just live and occupy space but we should feel an overwhelming duty to do something. Each person should ask him or herself the question that the eighteenth century philosopher Immanuel Kant asked: "What can I do?" Methuselah lived "nine hundred sixty nine years and died" (Genesis 5:27). It's interesting that nothing else is recorded about Methuselah who is reportedly the oldest man in the bible. It is true that the time and place of a person's life are the time and place of the body. However, the meaning and significance of that life, the strong influence that it has, and the impact that it makes can be far and wide. So it isn't how long one lives, but how well. Jesus died at 33 but in three years of his public ministry, he set in motion a movement that revolutionized the world. Joan of Arc died at 19 but she is famous for being a national military leader who served in France and tried to free that country from British control. King Tutankhamen, better known as "King Tut" became the ruler of Egypt at 9 and died at 18. He is one of the most famous kings of the eighteenth dynasty, during Egypt's "golden age." Alexander the Great was the general who conquered numerous territories and made Persia one of the greatest empires in the Western world. He died at 30. The English poet John Keats died at 26 and another English poet Percy Shelly at 30. The Scottish poet Robert Burns at 37, the English playwright Christopher Marlowe at 29, the American poet, Paul Laurence Dunbar at 34, John F. Kennedy at 46, and Martin Luther King, Jr. at 39. However, their short lives did not diminish their contributions.

Also, young people can make a difference. For example, Johann Wolfgang von Goethe and Victor Hugo were excellent writers at 20. Lord Roger Bacon began to philosophize at 16. Julius Caesar began his career at 17. Galilee was 18 when he saw the principle of the pendulum in the swinging lamps at the Cathedral of Pisa. Rembrandt was famous at 24, Mozart, Mendolssohn, Schubert and Beethovan produced music at 20, Booker T. Washington was the spokesperson for black America at 30. Countee Cullen and Langston Hughes wrote brilliant poems in their twenties. However, Methuselah lived "nine hundred sixty nine years and died." It's not how long one lives, but how well. Proverbs 3 says: "My child do not forget my teaching, but let your heart keep my commandments, for length of days and years of life, and abundant welfare they will give you." The popular poem "Bridge Builder" comes to mind:

> An old man, going a lone highway,
> Came, at the evening, cold and gray,
> To a chasm, vast, and deep, and wide,
> Through which was flowing a sullen tide.
> The old man crossed in the twilight dim; the sullen stream
>   had no fears for him; but he turned, when safe on the
>   other side, and built a bridge to span the tide.
> "Old man," said a fellow pilgrim, near,
> "You are wasting strength with building here; Your jour-
>   ney will end with the ending day; You never again will

pass this way; You have crossed the chasm, deep and wide—Why build a bridge at the eventide?"

The builder lifted his old gray head:

"Good friend, in the path I have come," he said, "There will come after me today, [Young people] whose feet must pass this way.

This chasm, that has been naught to me,

To [them] may a pitfall be. [They], too, must cross in the twilight dim; Good friend, I'm building the bridge for [them]."

Trust in the Lord

MRS. ANNIE MAE NIX

"Trust in the Lord with all thine heart; and lean not unto thine own understanding. In all your ways acknowledge him, and he shall direct thy paths."
— Proverbs 3:5–6

The book of Proverbs is one of the wisdom books of the Old Testament. It contains instructions on many of the practical matters of daily life. It points the believer to God with instructions on how to live a holy and upright life. Most scholars believe that Solomon wrote Proverbs but not all of Proverbs. However, many people during Solomon's time were not trusting and depending on God. They took pride in their own achievements, intellect and understanding. We have this same problem today. Many people in our time are not trusting and depending on God. For a better idea of trusting and depending on God, I would like to share with you three points.

Point One is "Trust God." Point Two is "Acknowledge

God." Point Three is "Lean Not on Your Own Under-standing."

Let's look briefly at Point One. To me, "trust in God" means believing and depending on God in spite of problems, trials and tribulations. I am not shaken because of bad reports. I have chosen to believe the Lord's good report. Bad news does not affect me the same way as it used to. I have learned how to trust and believe God's Word. Hebrews 13:5 says: "I will never leave thee nor forsake thee." Personally, in 1994, I was facing what seemed to be a likely death sentence. The doctors said that I only had six months to live. However, I have not let what doctors say stop me from living. I enjoy each day and maintain a quality of life. I have put my trust in God and, like others, I know that my life is ultimately in His hands. The Hebrew boys trusted God in a fiery furnace (Daniel 3:19–24). Daniel trusted him in the lion's den. (Daniel 5:19–24). Job trusted him in spite of losing everything in one day (Job 1:13–22). Job stated: "The Lord gave and the Lord has taken away, blessed be the name of the Lord" (Job 1:21). Nevertheless, it is important to trust God during good times and during bad times. I am determined to trust in God.

Second, we must "acknowledge God." To "acknowledge God" means to give God praise, glory and honor. David acknowledged God by saying in Psalm 23: "The Lord is my Shepherd; I shall not want." David also said in Psalm 27: "The Lord is my light and my salvation; whom shall

I fear? The Lord is the strength of my life; whom shall I be afraid."However, we must acknowledge God in our daily walk and talk.

Third, in order to trust God, we must lean not on our own understanding. Our own understanding is doing what we want to do and not following God's Word. If we love God we will obey and keep His commandments. Saint John 14:15 says: "If ye love me, keep my commandments." Joseph's brothers were leaning on their understanding when they threw Joseph in the pit. Judas Iscariot was leaning on his own understanding when He betrayed Jesus for thirty pieces of silver. Aaron was leaning on his own understanding and following the will of the people when He made a golden calf instead of adhering to God's command in Exodus 20:4 which says: "Thou shalt not make unto thee any graven image, or any likeness of anything, that is in heaven above or that is in the earth beneath, or that is in the water under the earth."

I would like for you to remember three things from the text: (1) Trust in God, (2) Acknowledge God, and (3) Lean not on your own understanding. Proverbs 3:5–6 says: "Trust in the Lord with all thine heart; and lean not unto thine own understanding. In all your ways acknowledge him, and he shall direct thy paths."

In closing, God trusted Jesus and Jesus trusted God. God said: "This is my beloved Son in whom I am well-pleased" (Luke 3:22). God needed somebody to die for the sins of the world. Noah could not do it because after the flood he planted a vineyard, drank wine and was drunk (Genesis 9:21). Abraham could not do it because he said Sarah was his sister which was not true: "And Abraham said of Sarah, his wife, she is my sister" (Genesis 20:2). Moses could not do it because in Numbers 20:8–12, he was disobedient. However, there was only one that God could trust—His only begotten Son. The Scripture says that "God so loved the world, that he gave His only begotten Son, that whosoever believeth in Him shall not perish but have everlasting life." (John 3:16). Jesus died but he rose again with all *power* of heaven and earth in His hands . . . *power* to save . . . *power* to deliver . . . *power* to help and *power* to heal . . . *power* to make a way out of no way . . . *power* to deliver and *power* to set free . . .

I will trust in the Lord . . . I'm going to treat everybody right . . . I'm going to going to stay on the battlefield, until I die . . . Amen.

The Nix Family at Furman University,
Greenville, South Carolina

CPSIA information can be obtained at www.ICGtesting.com
Printed in the USA
LVOW130918040512

280359LV00001B/258/P